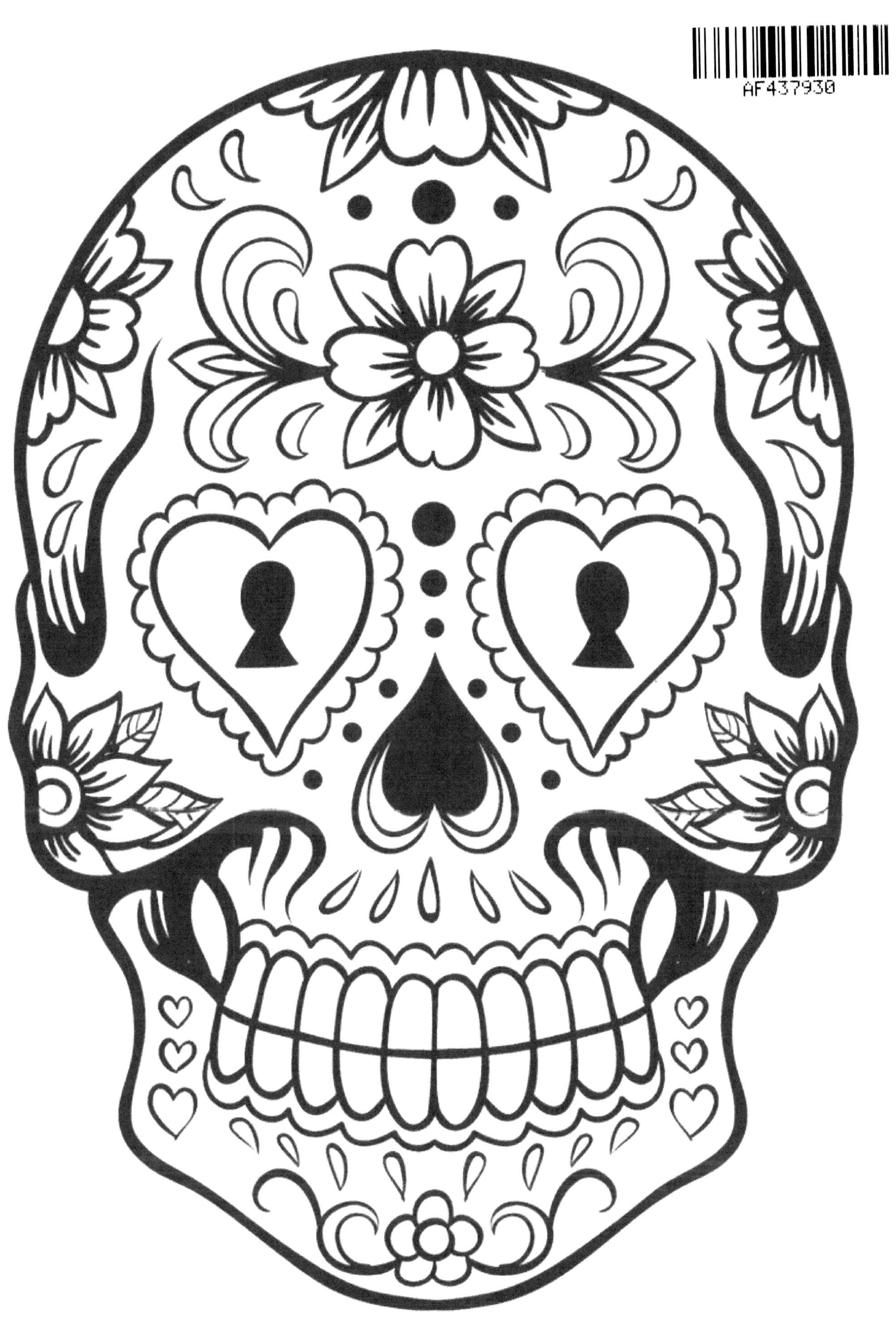
AF437930

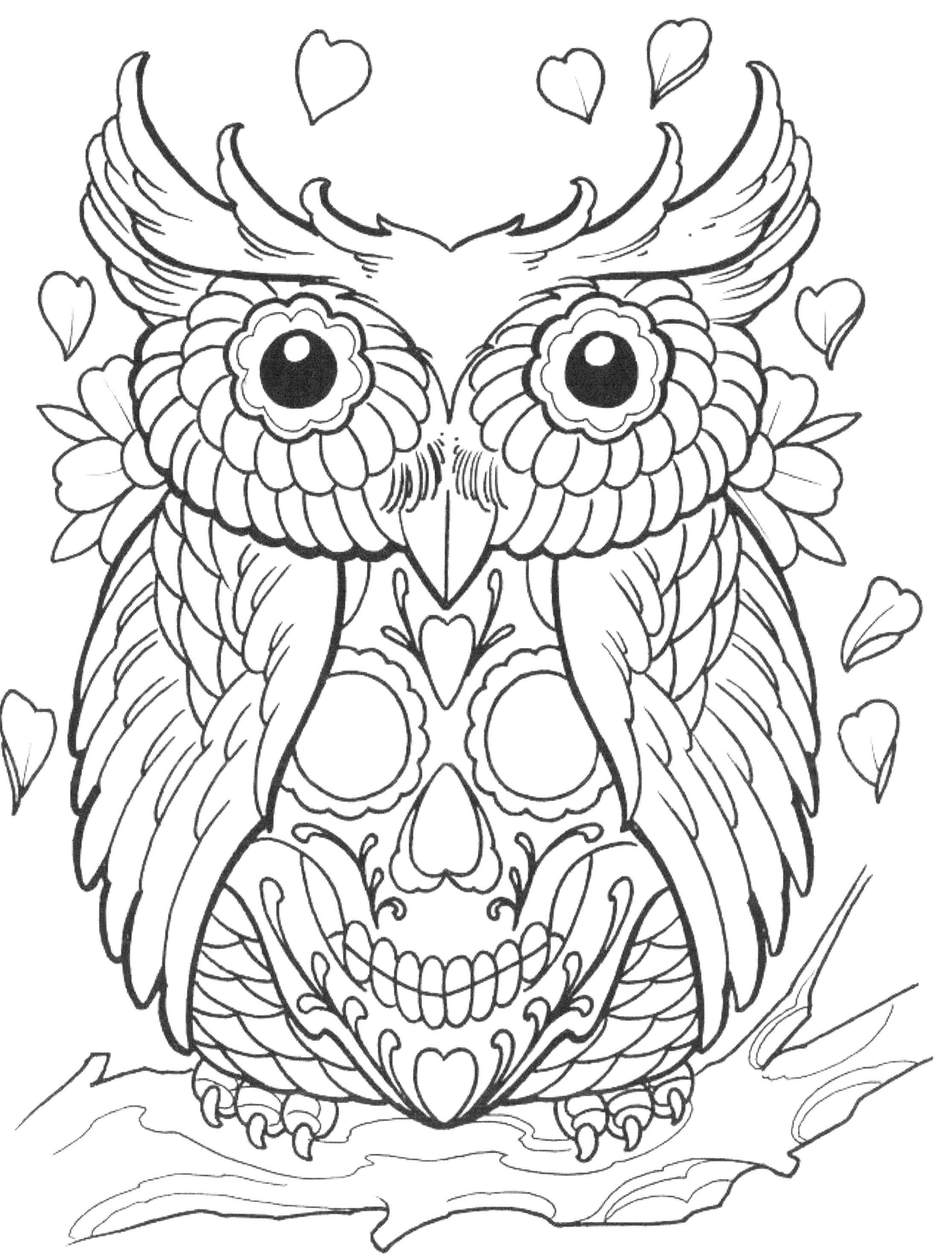

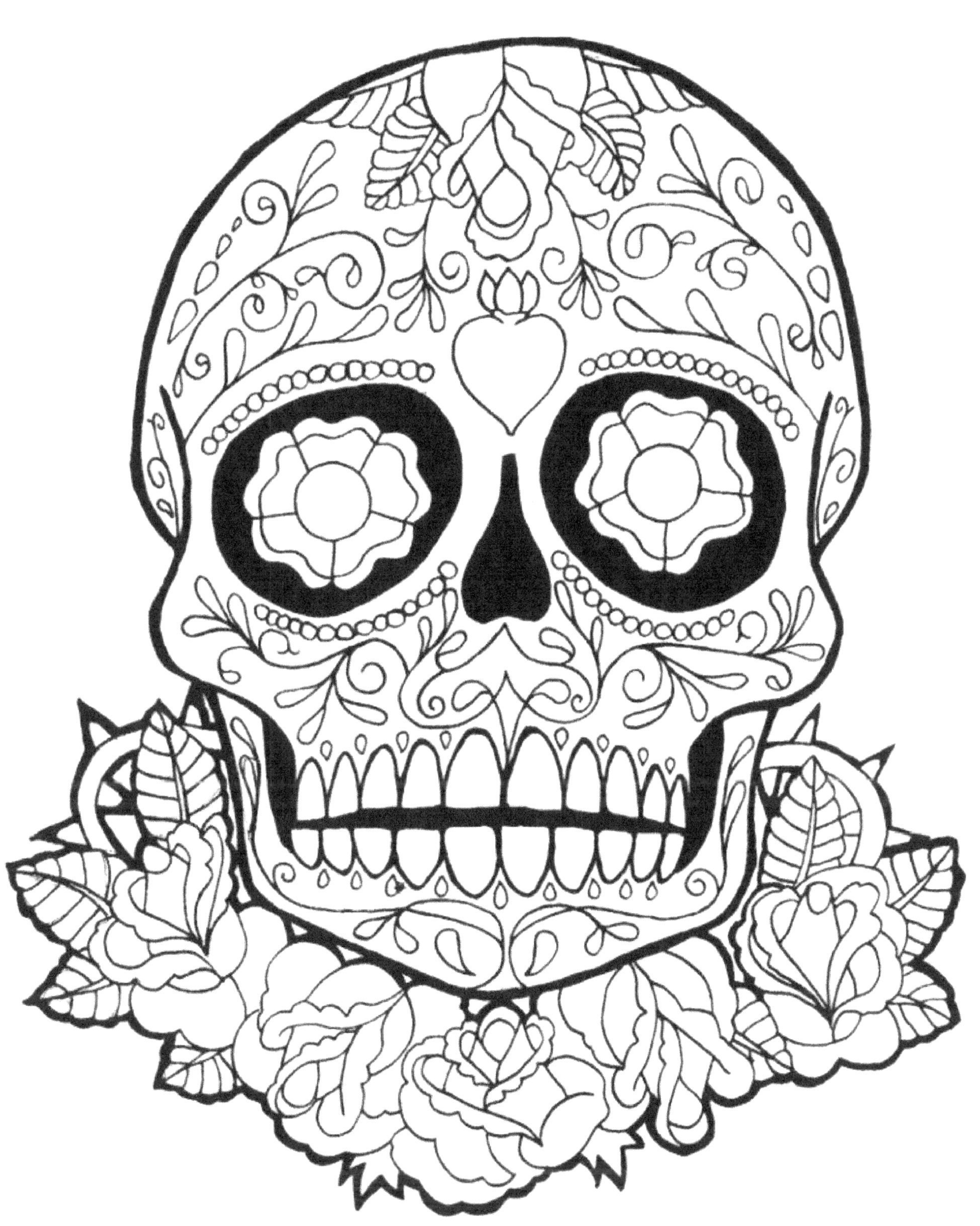

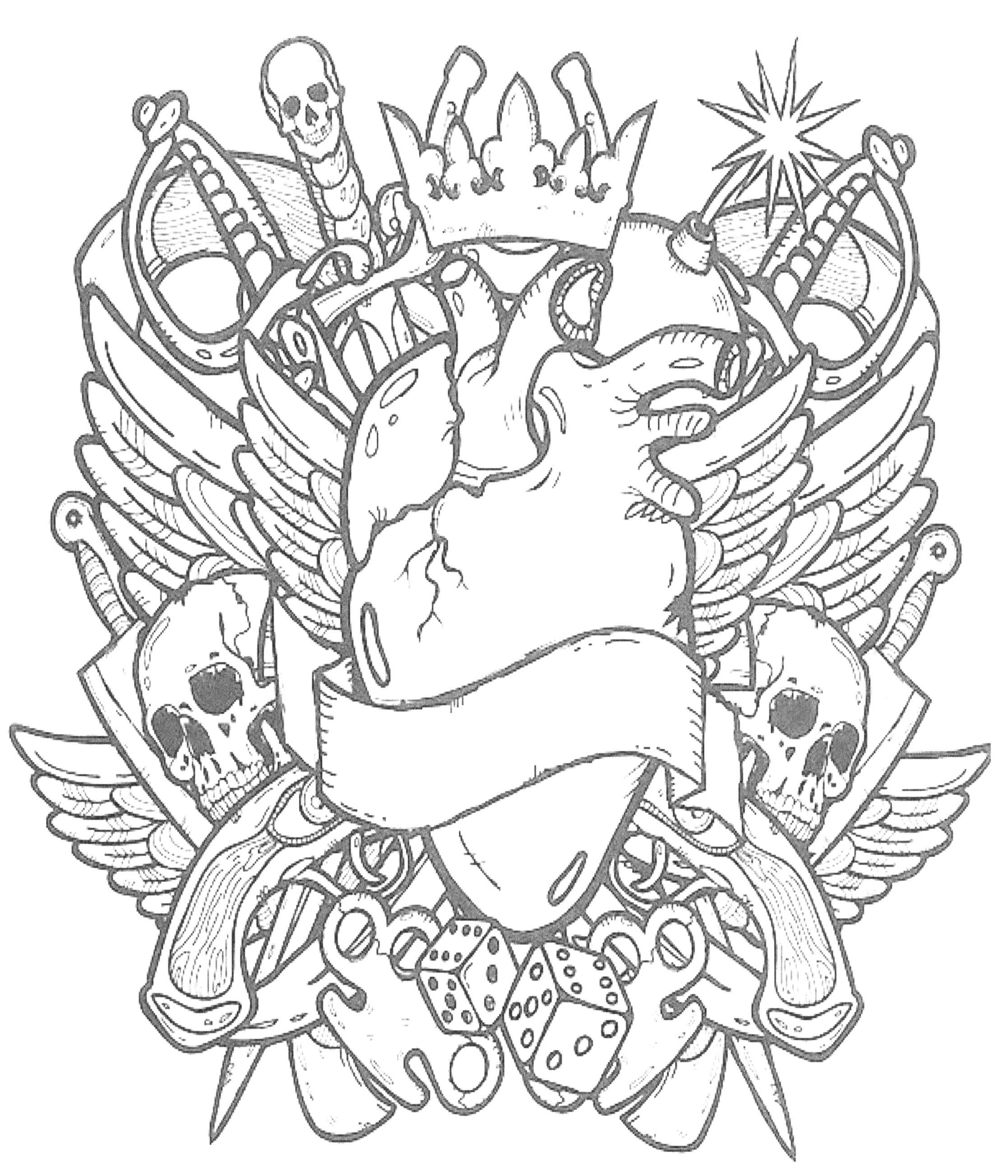

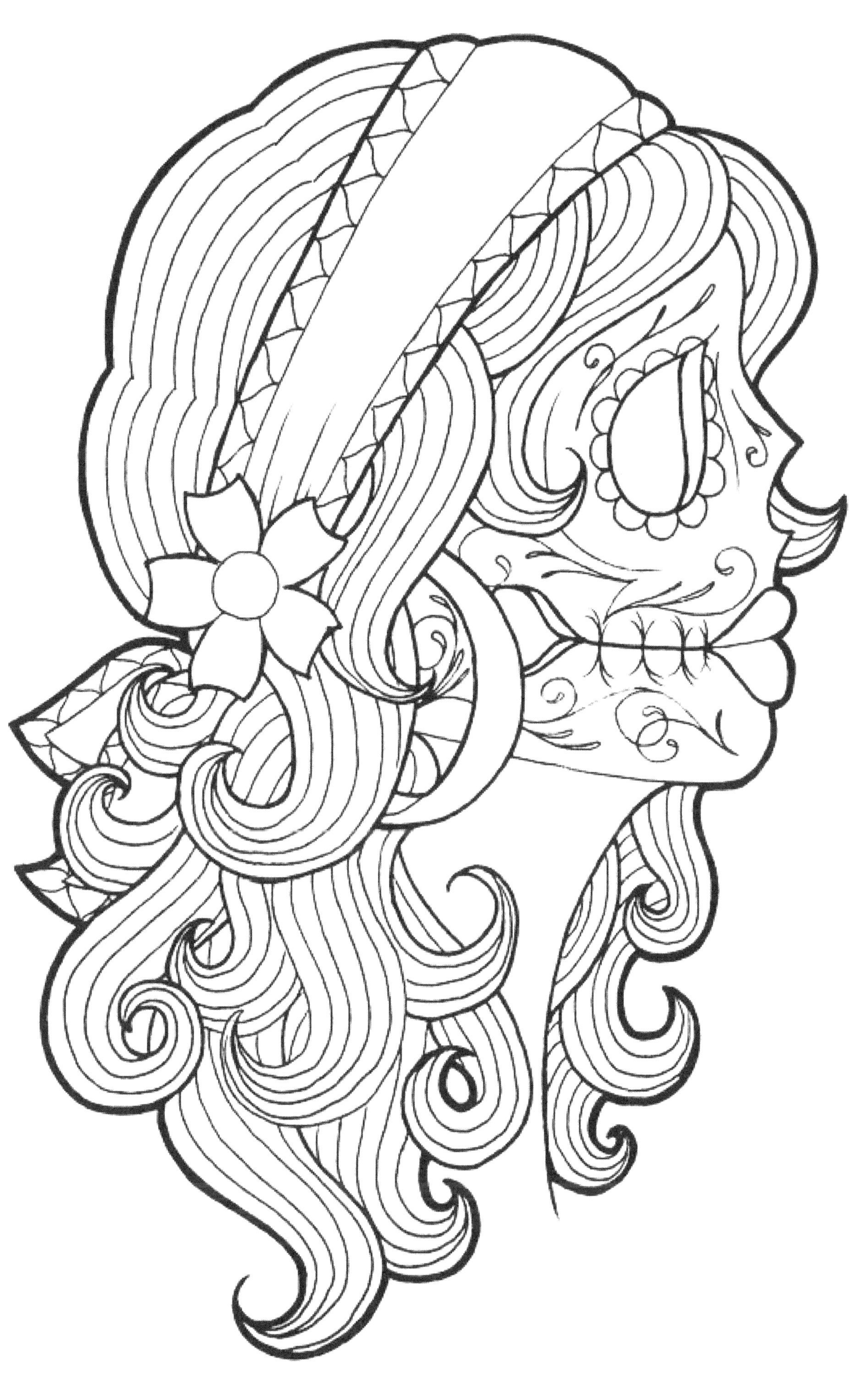

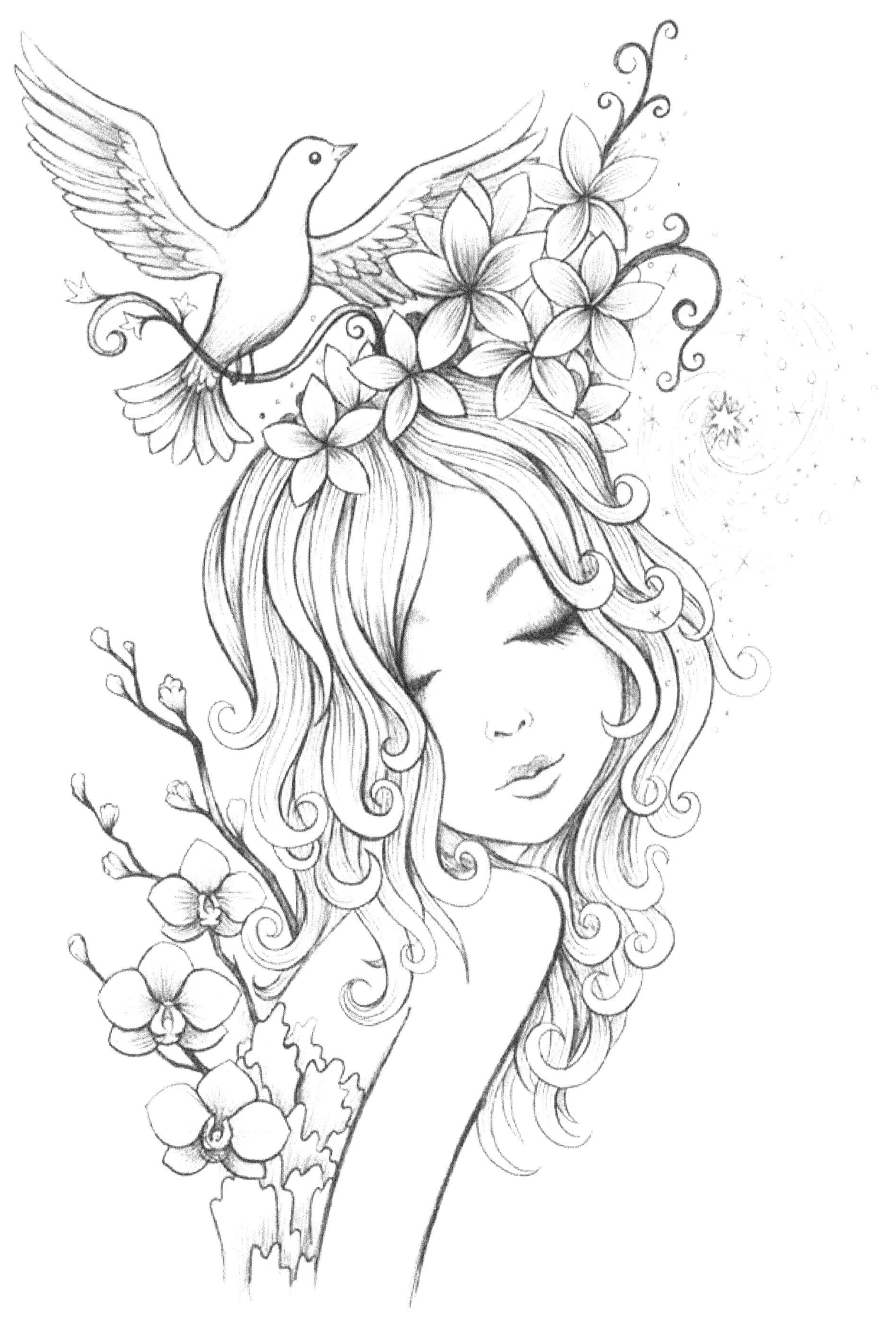

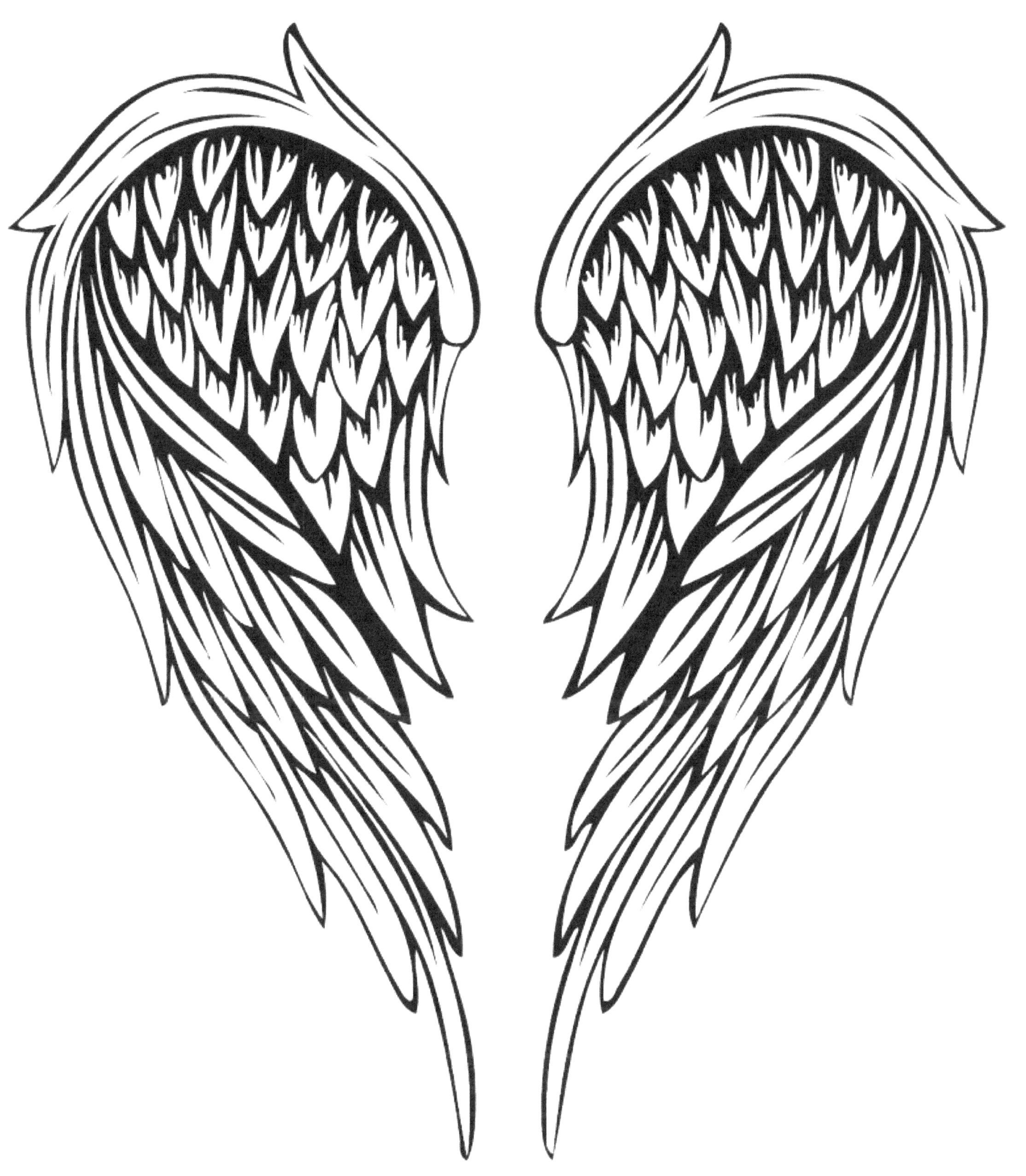

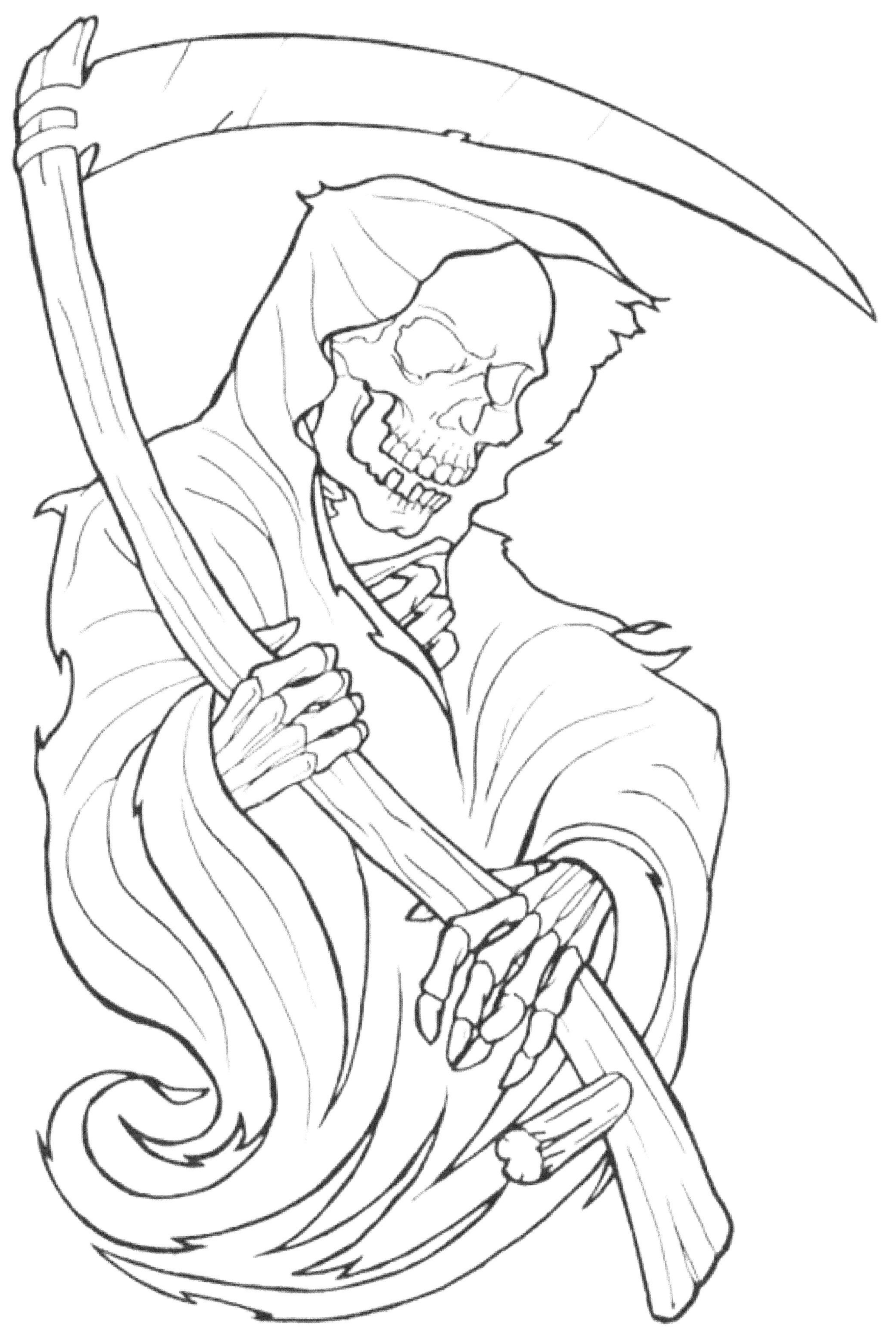

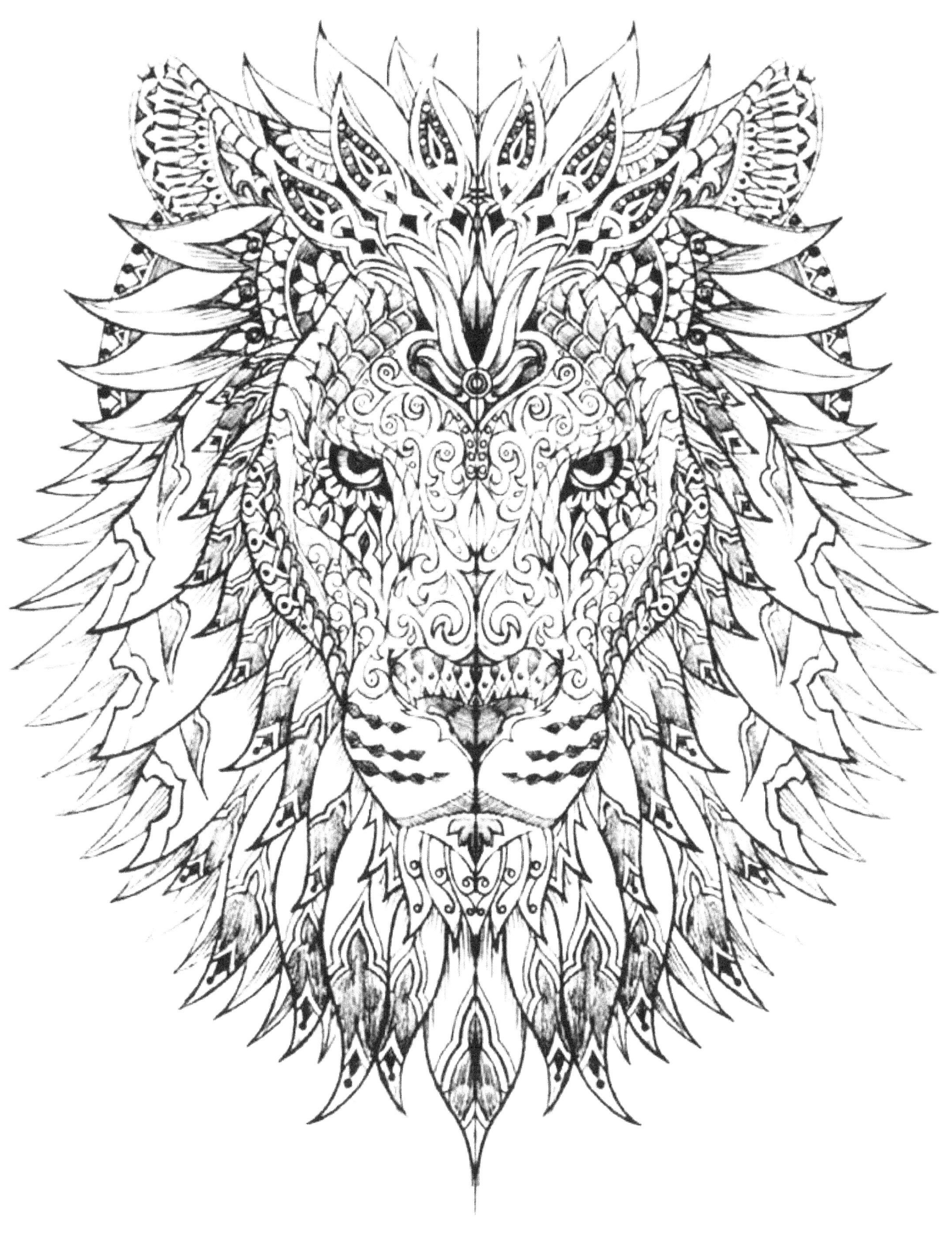

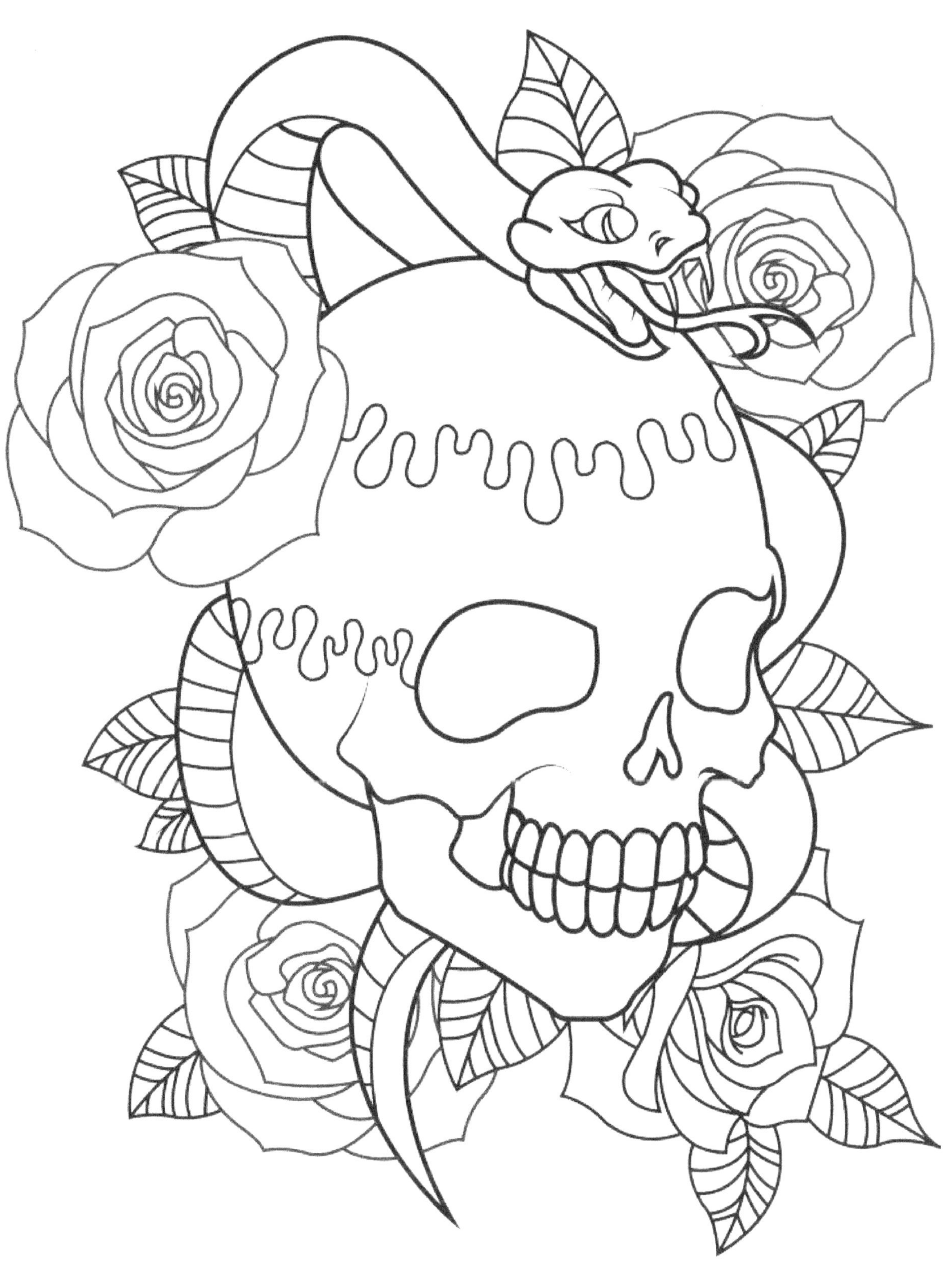

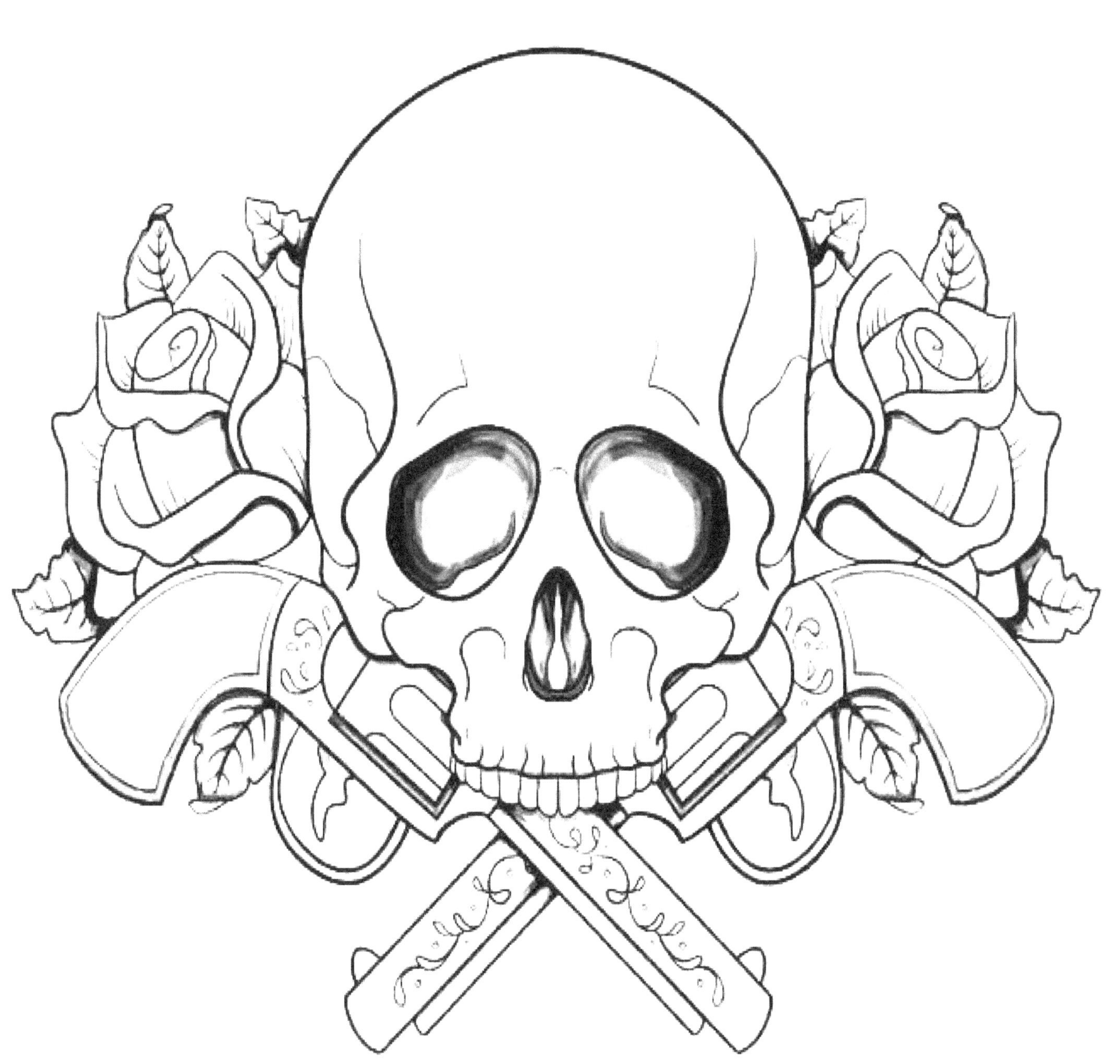

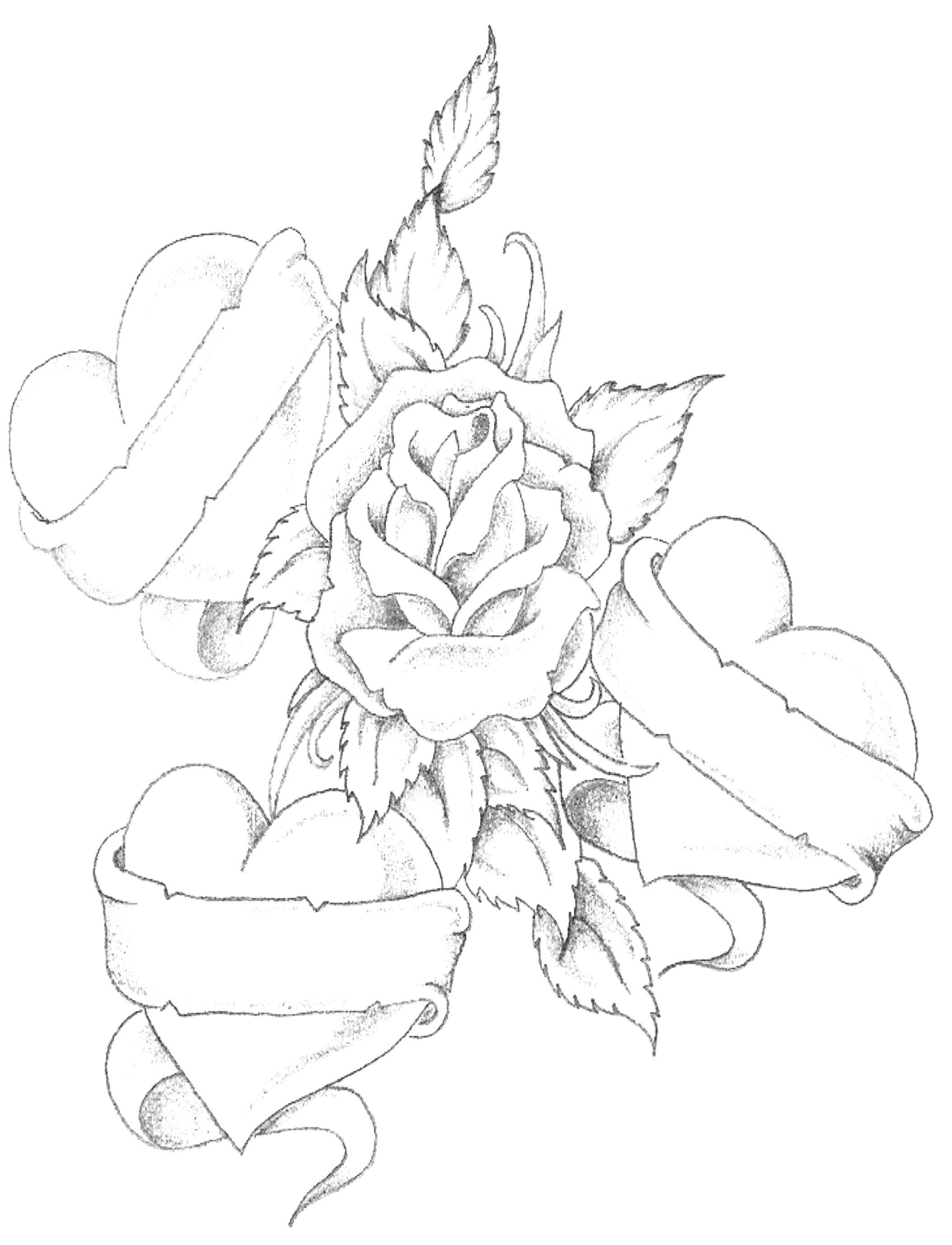

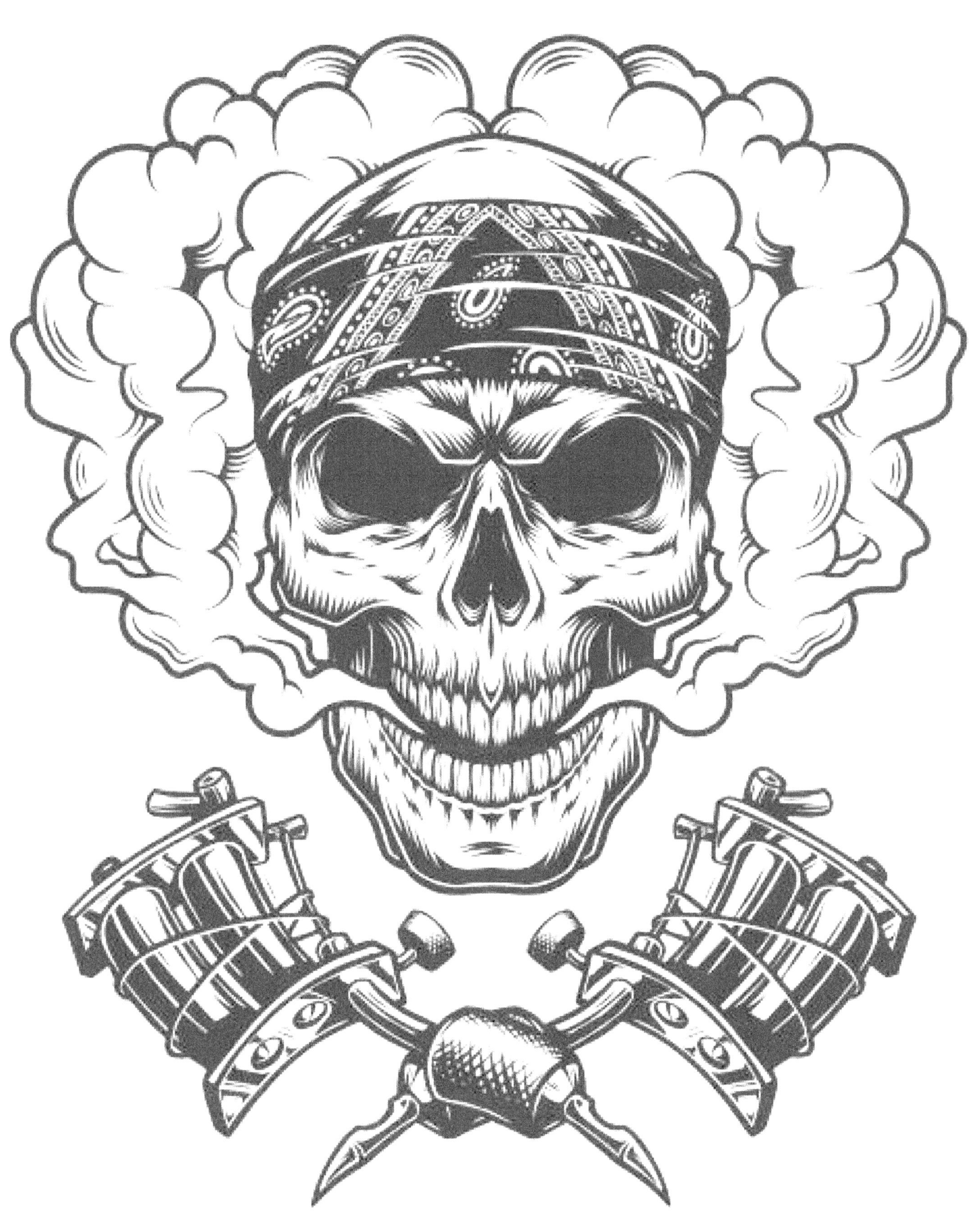

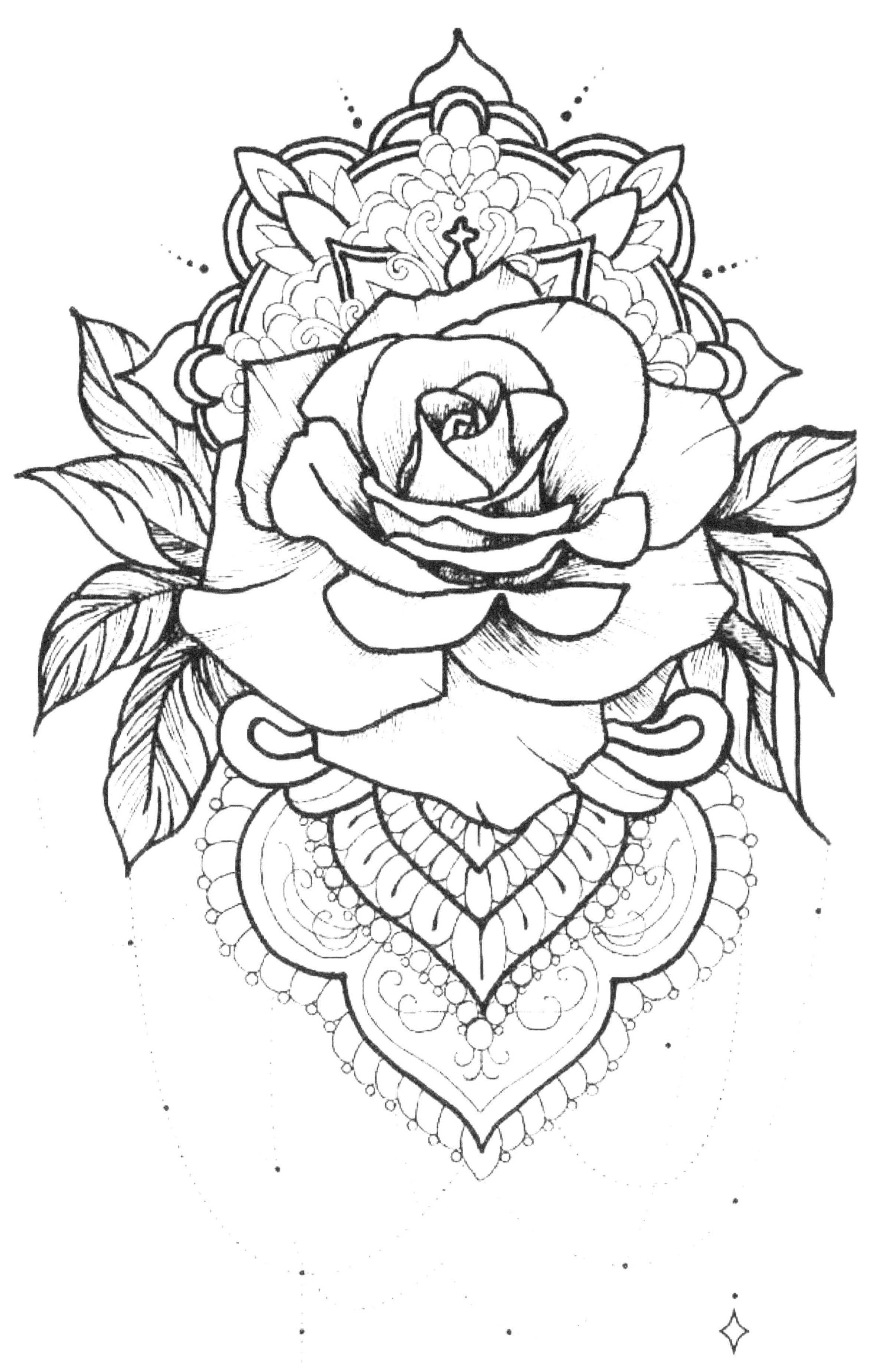

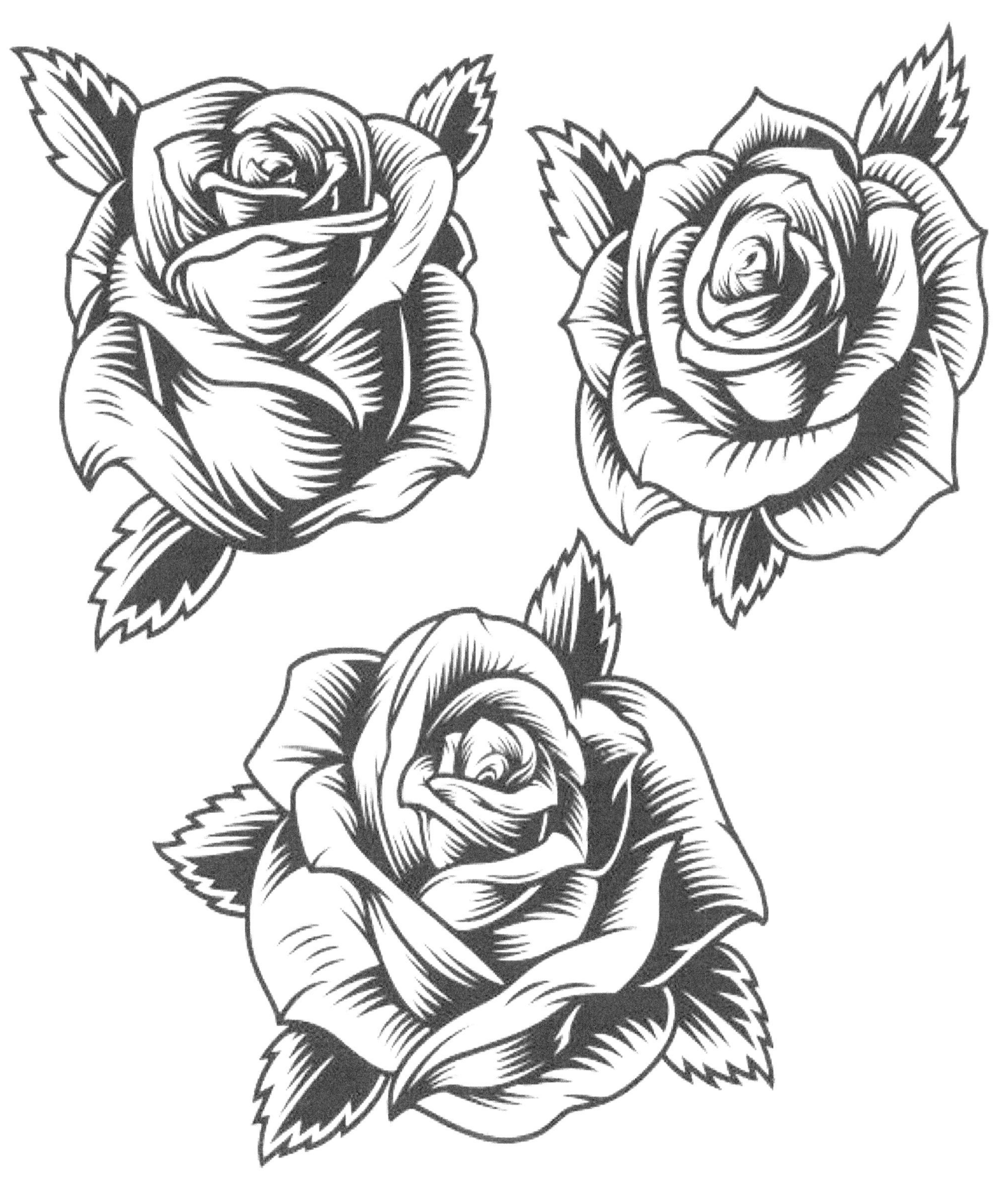

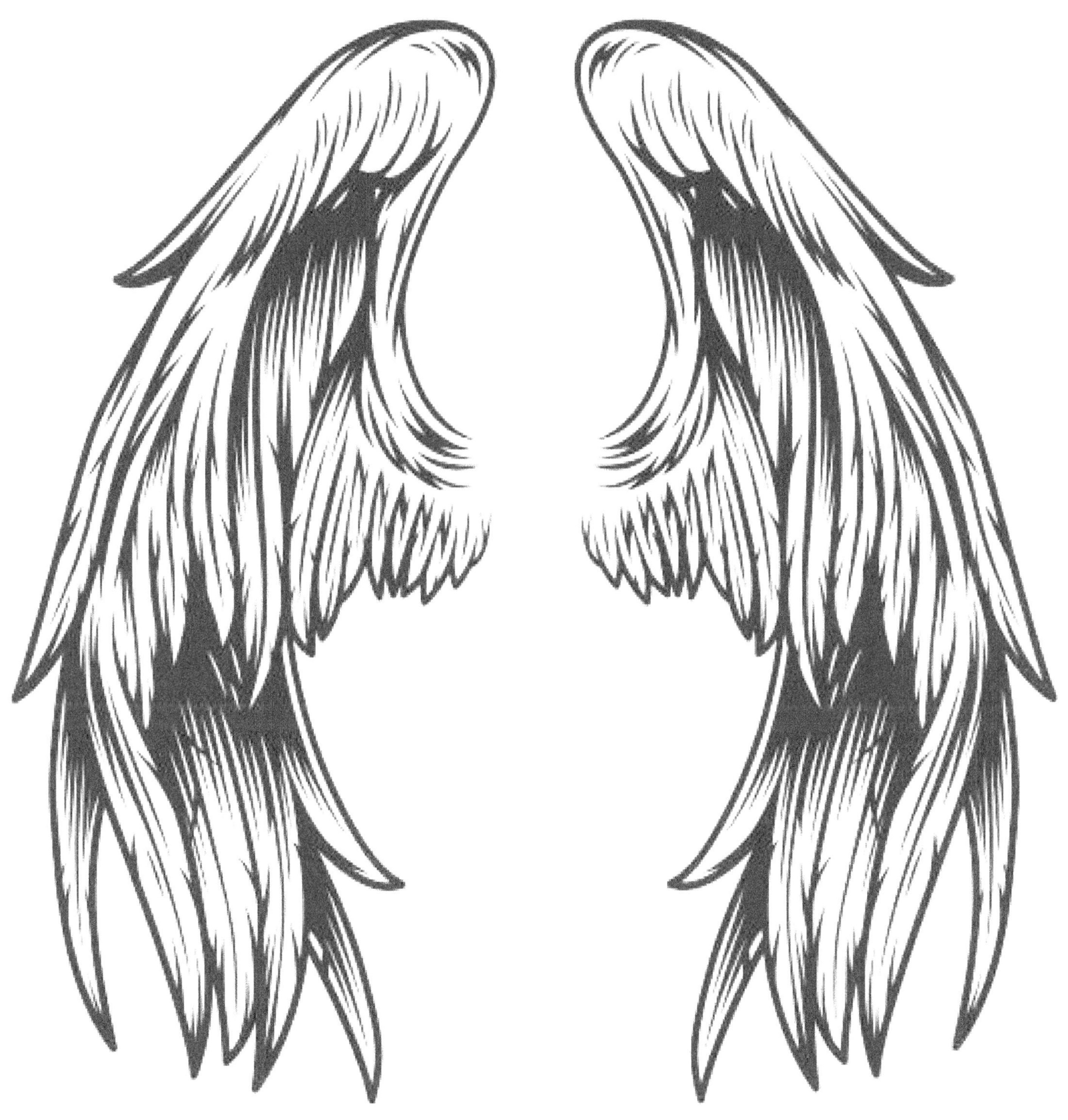

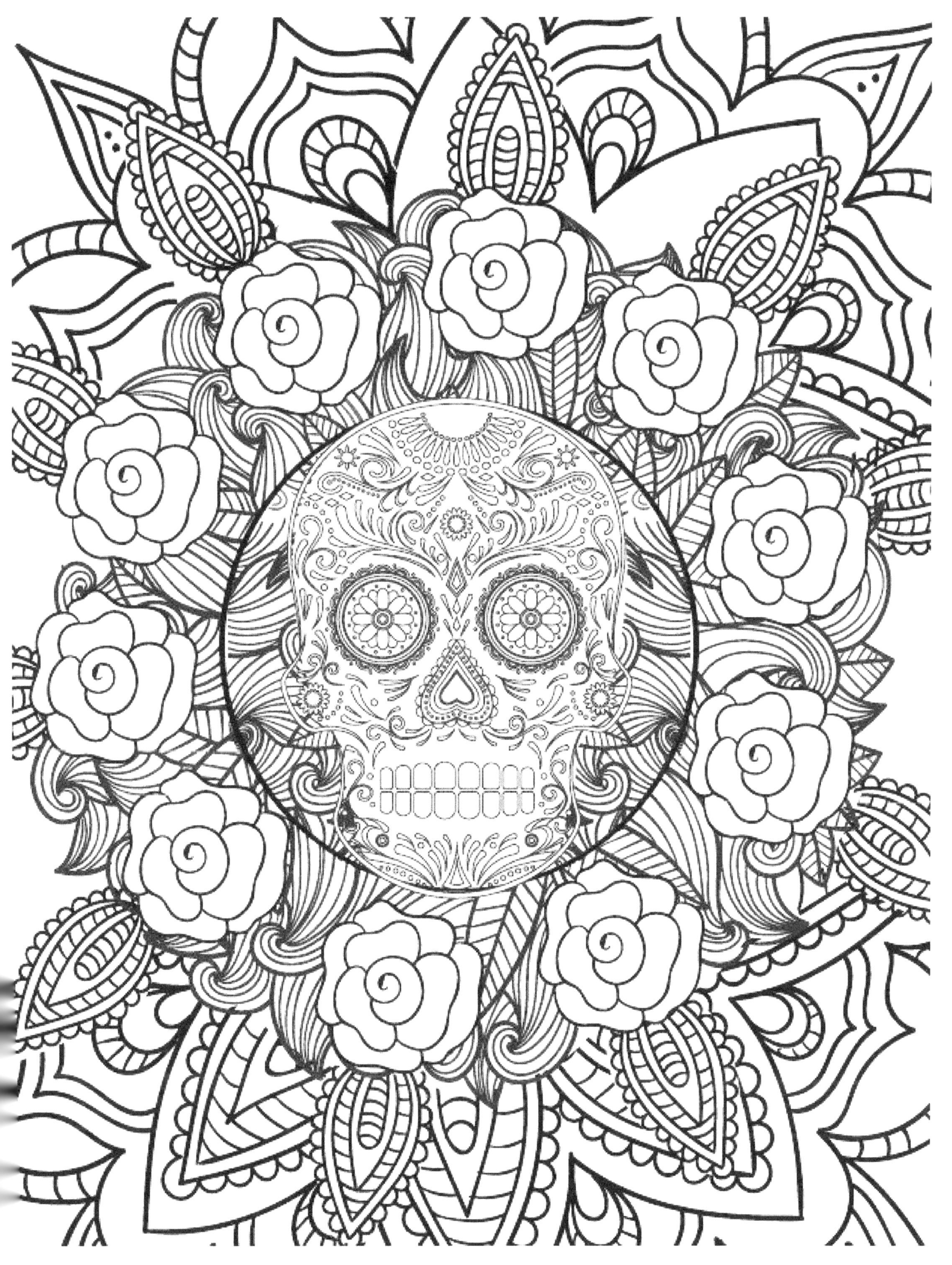

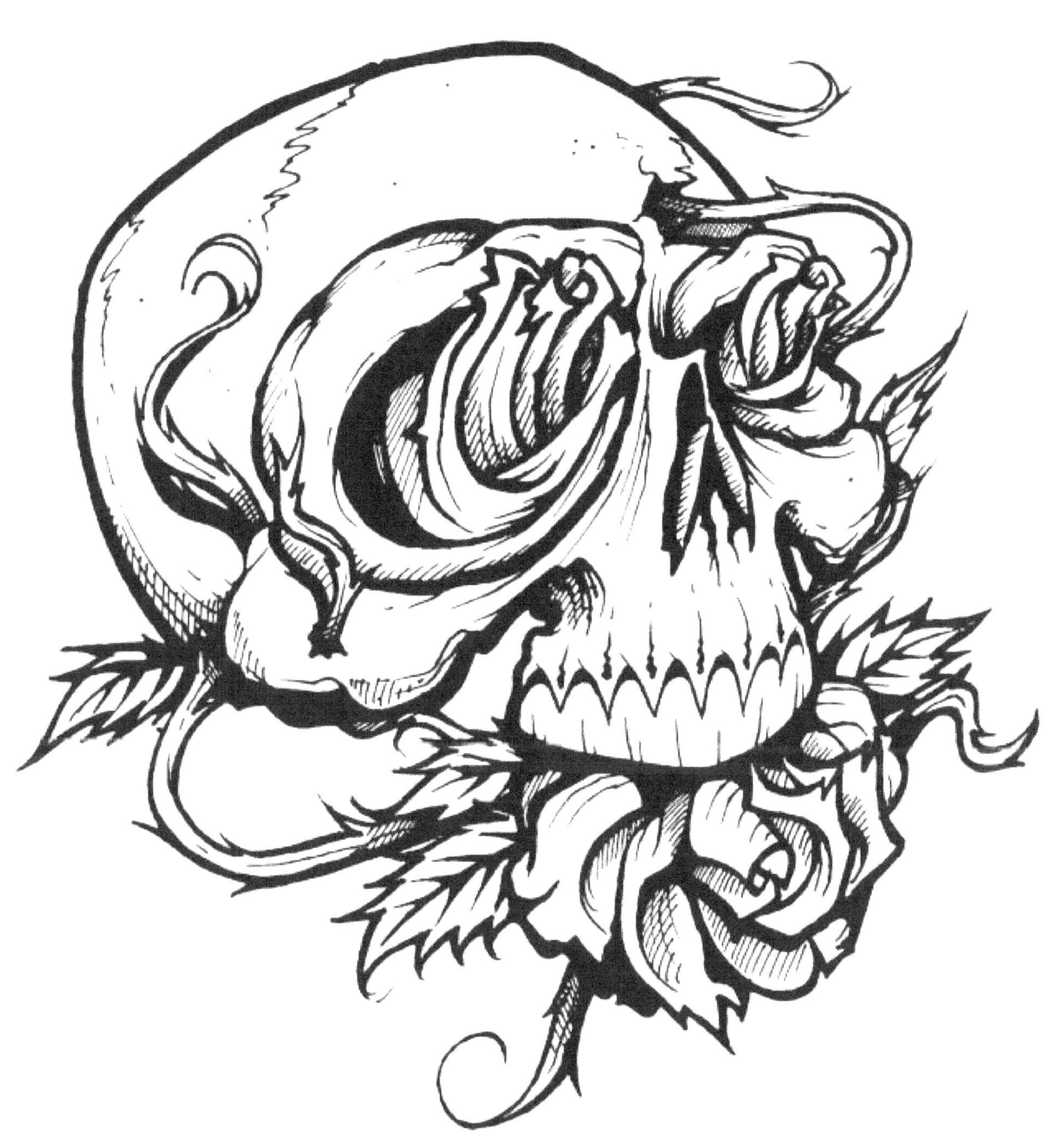

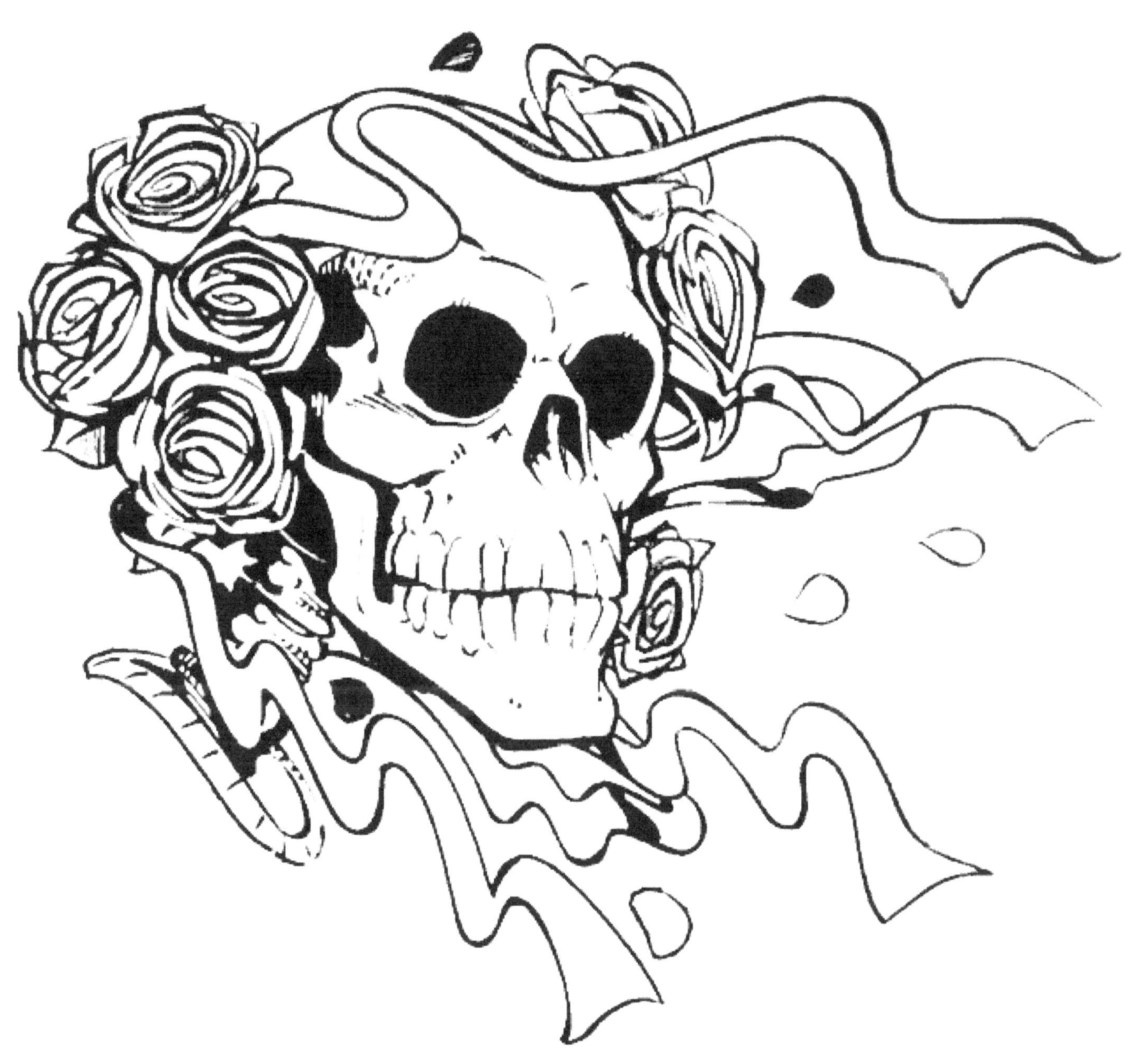

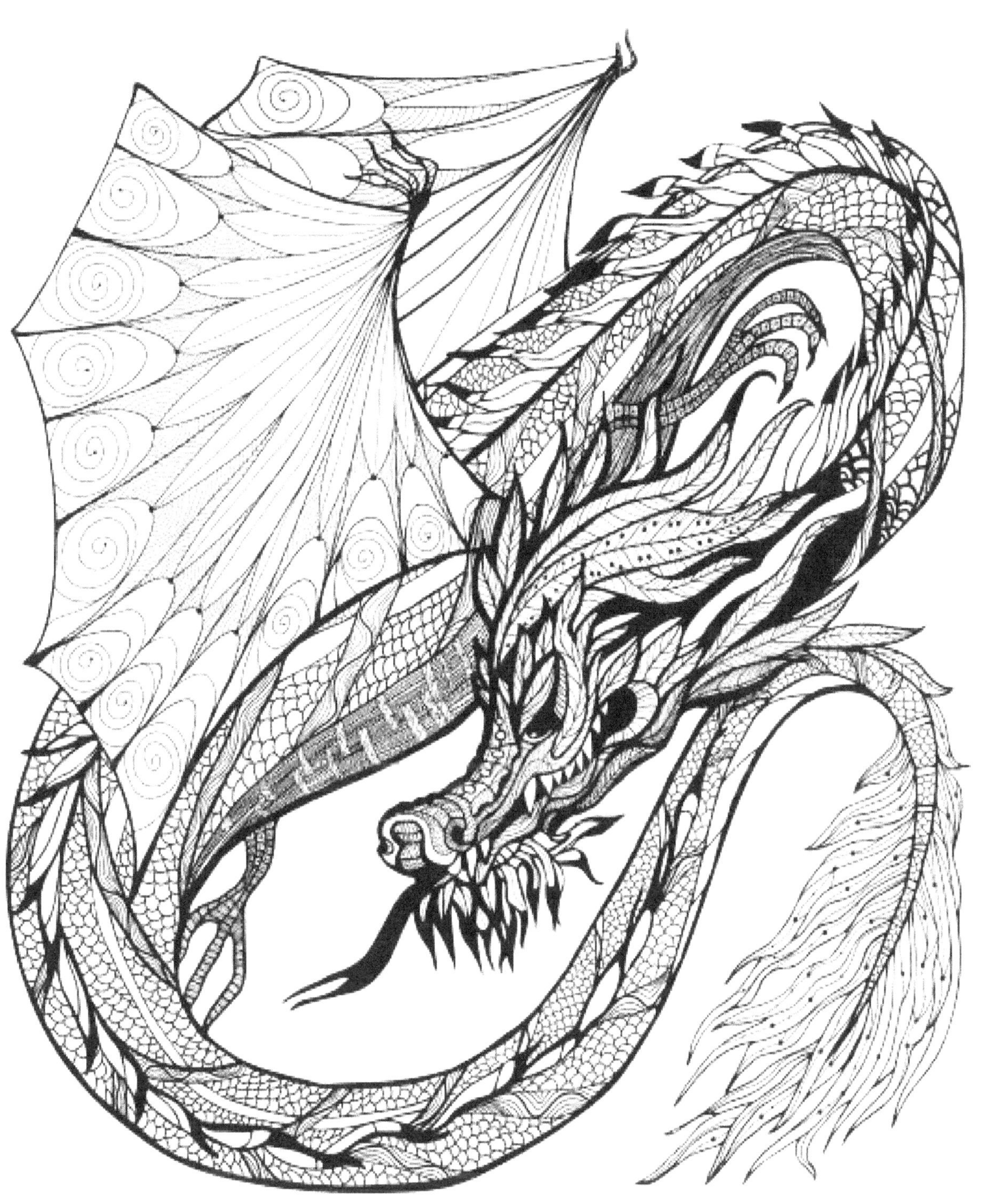

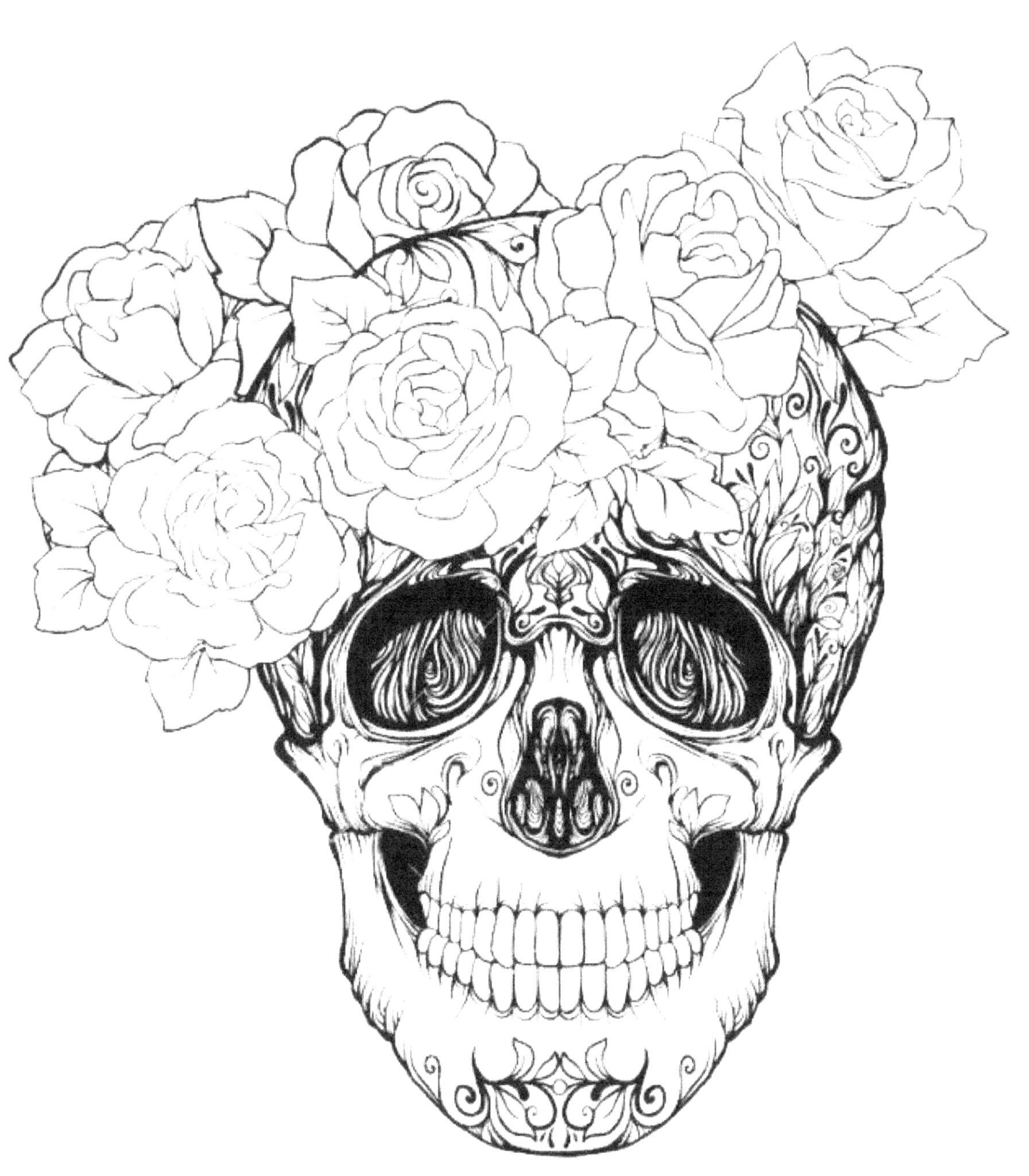

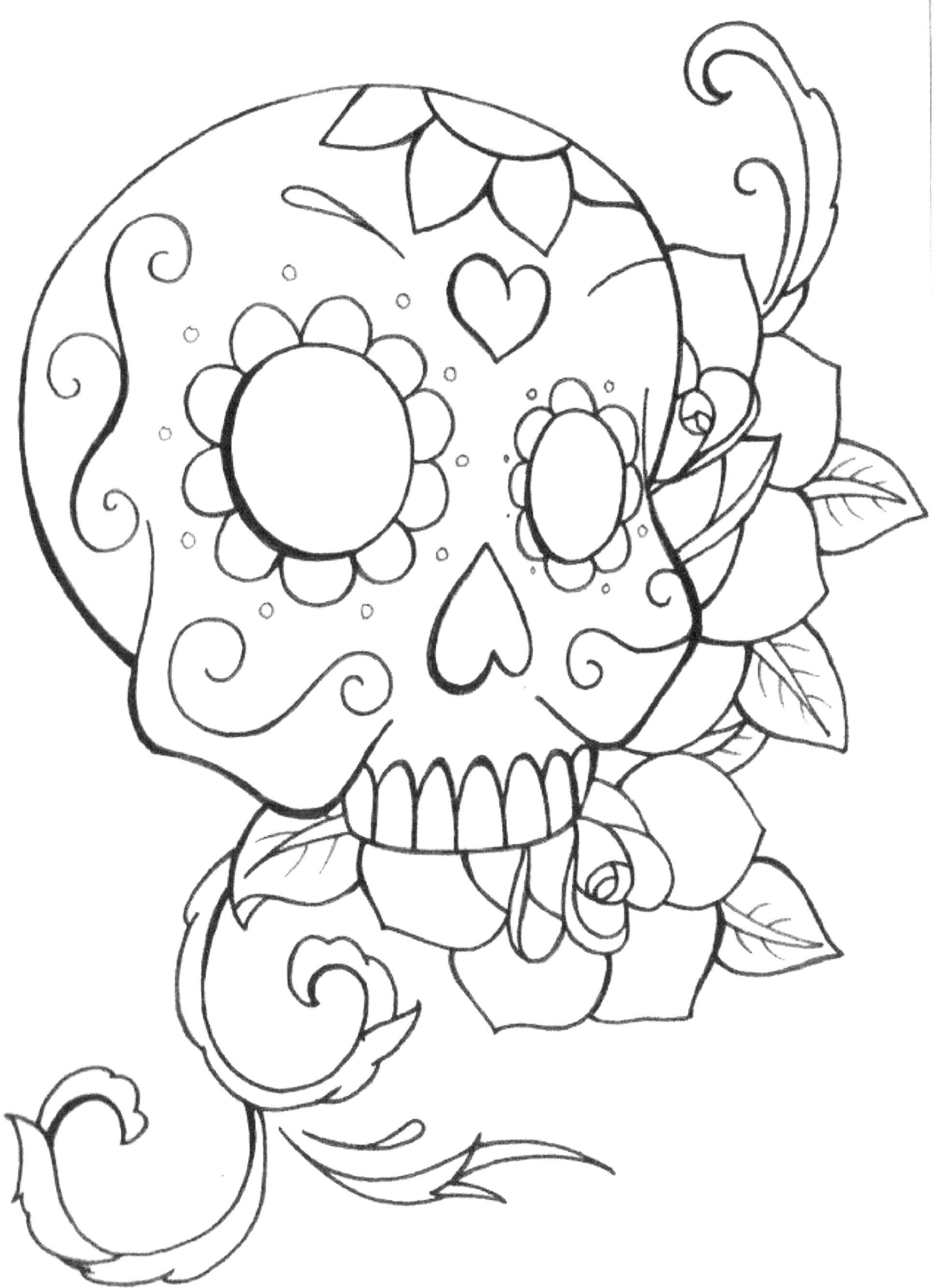

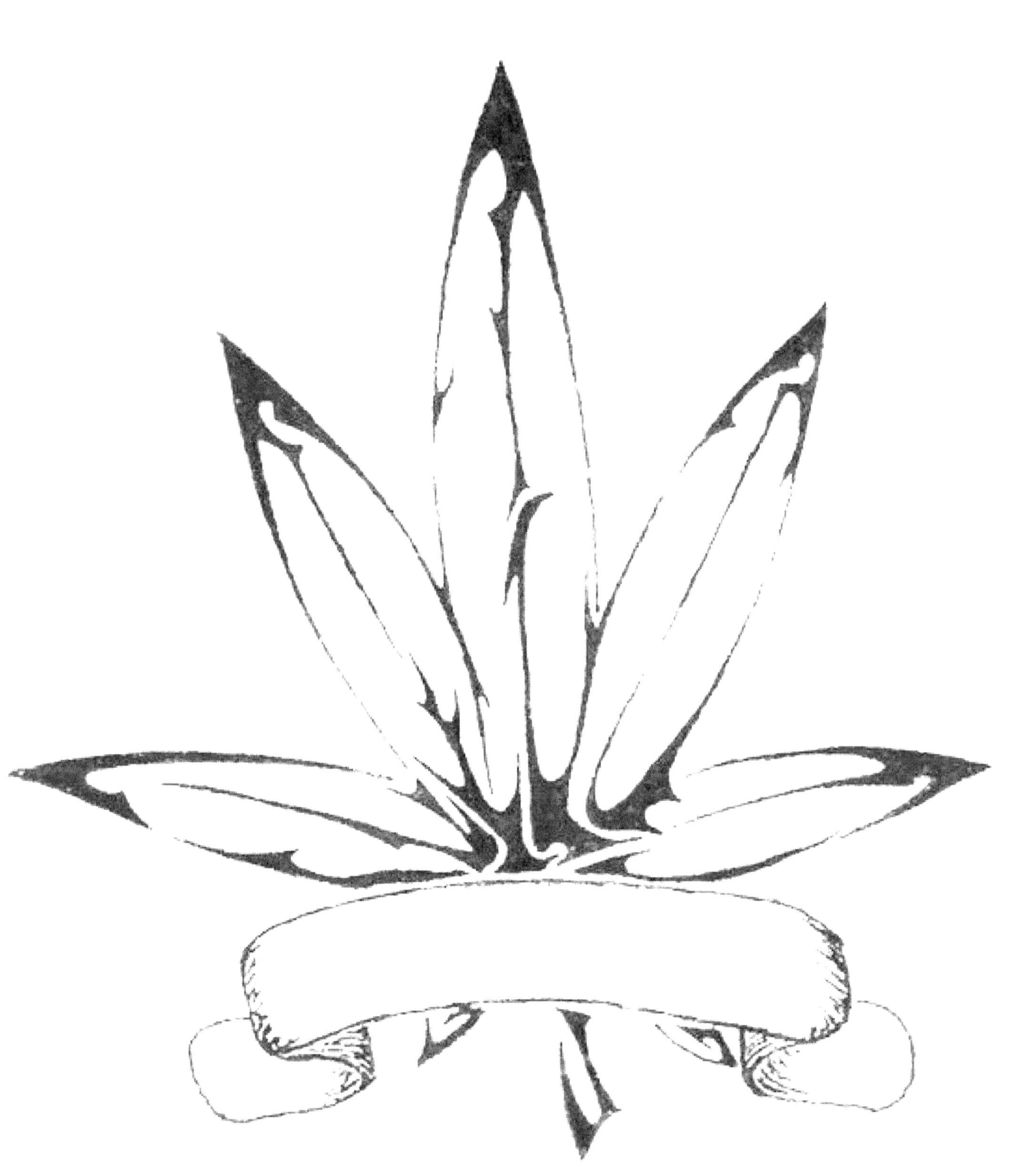

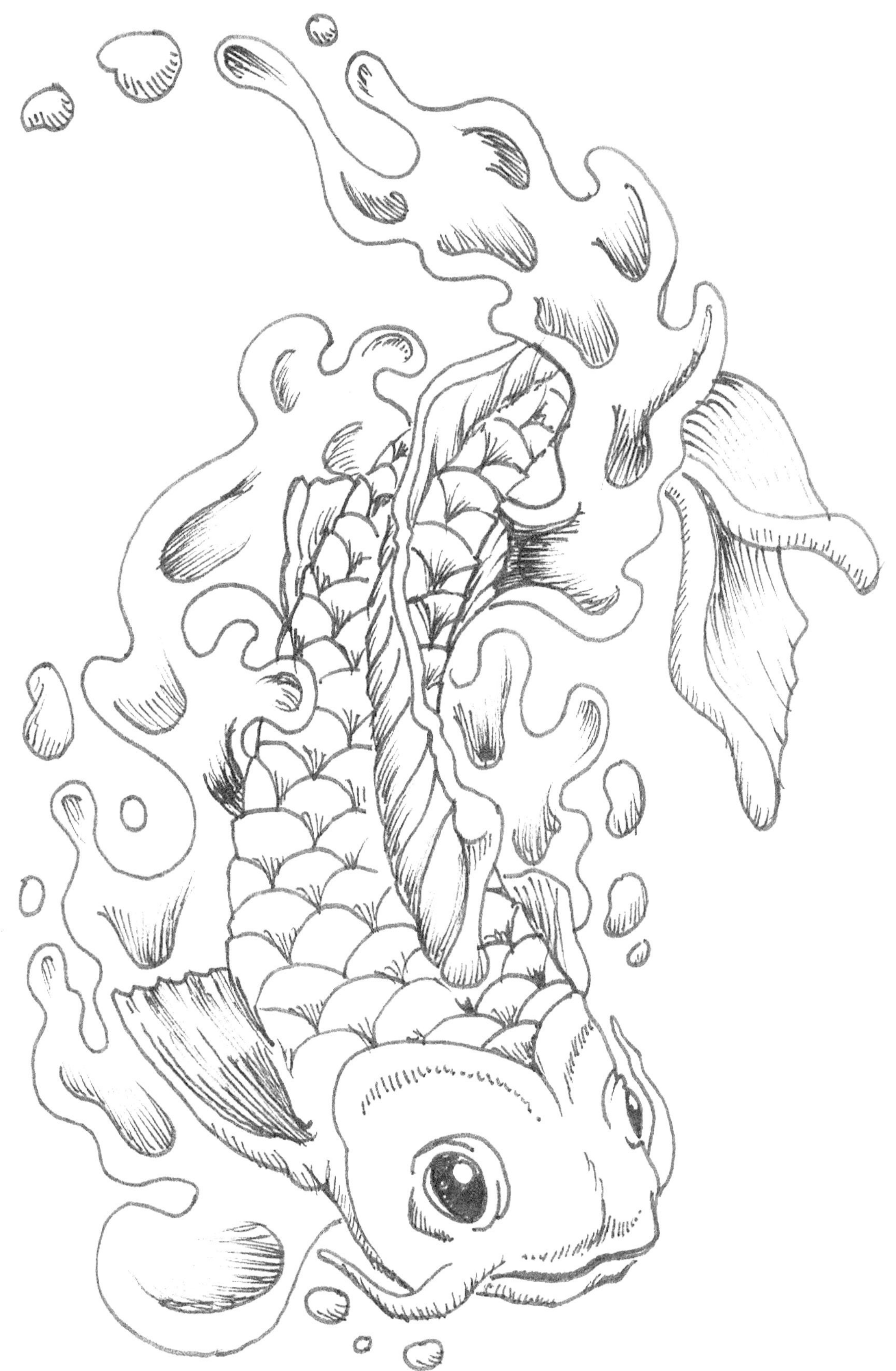

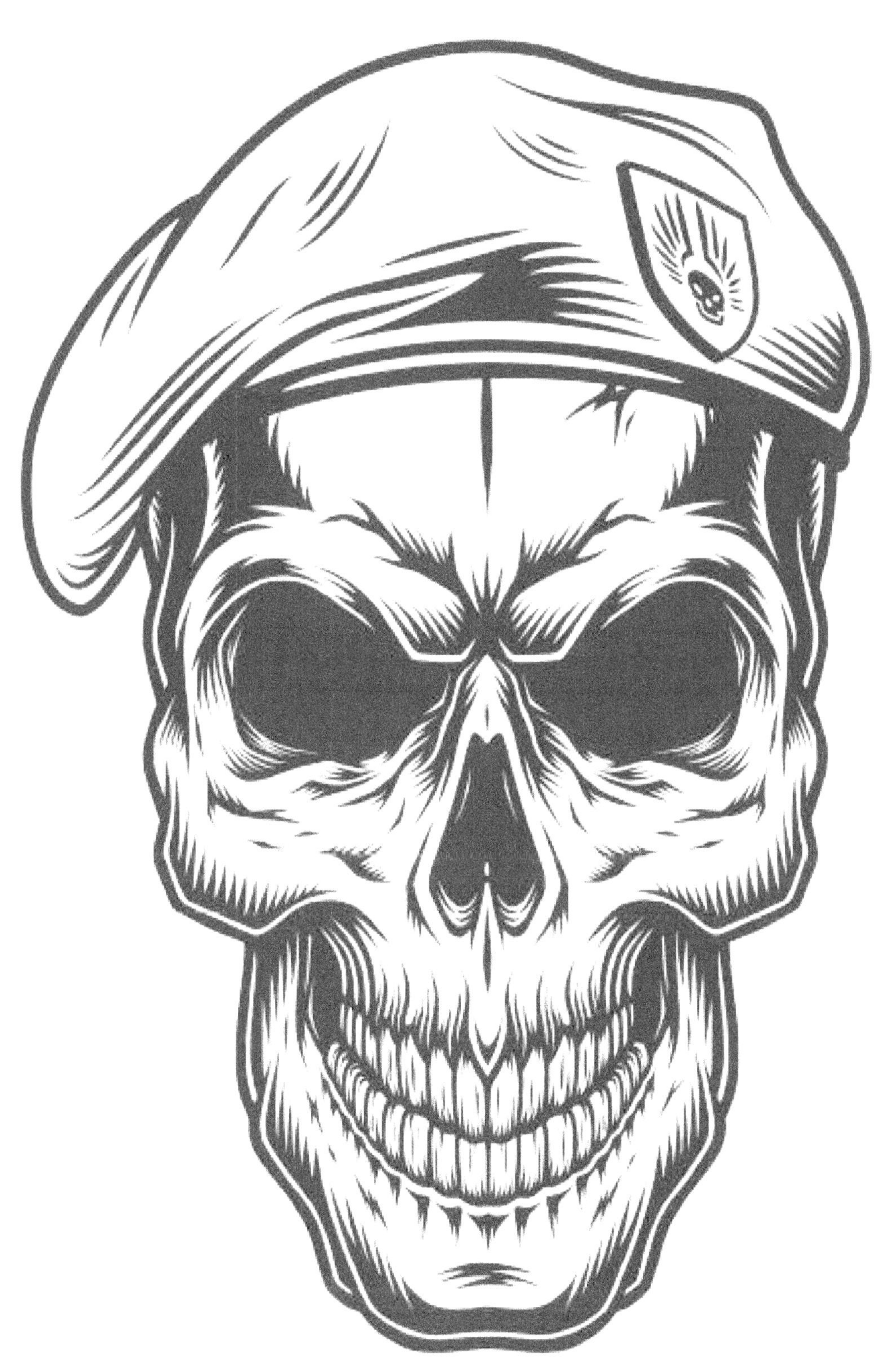

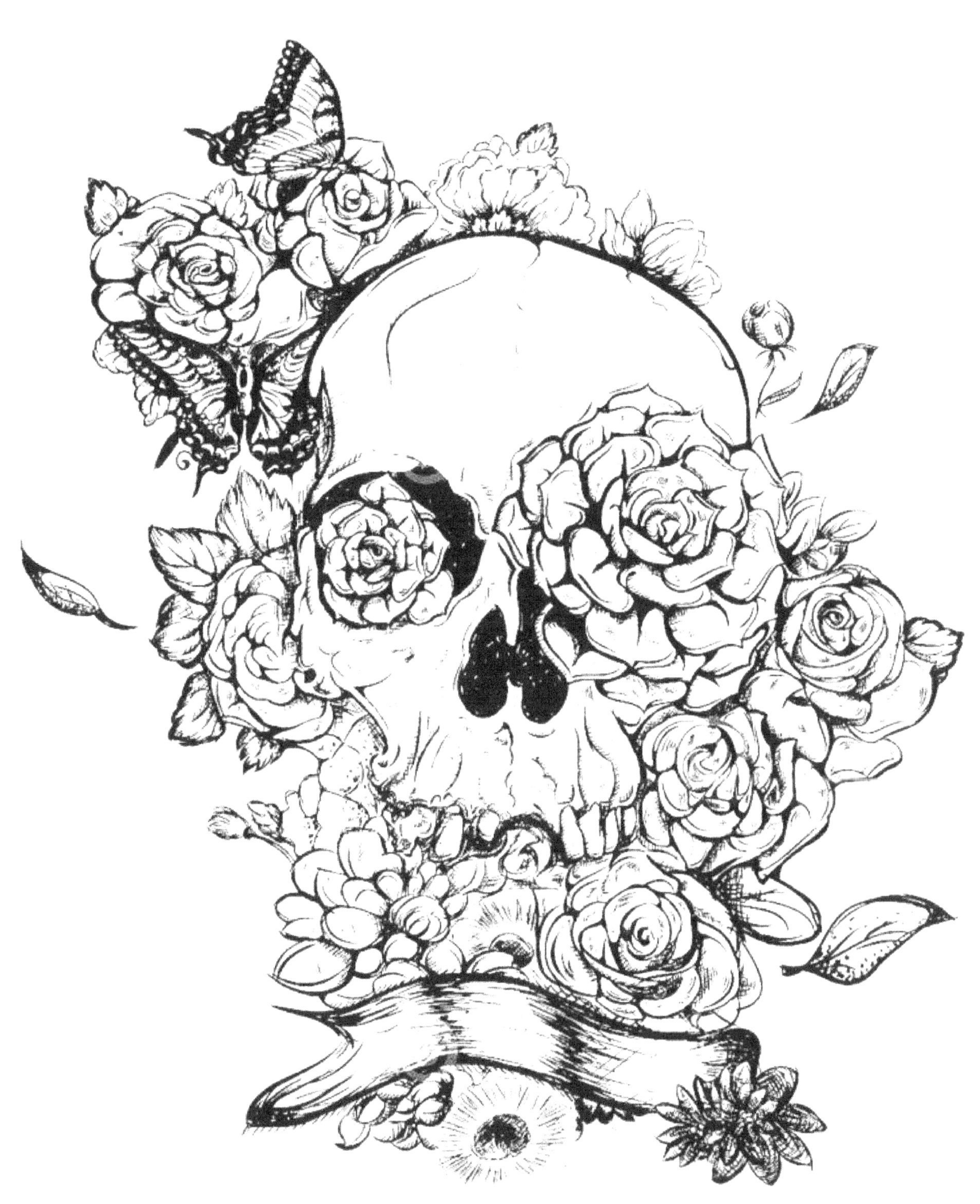

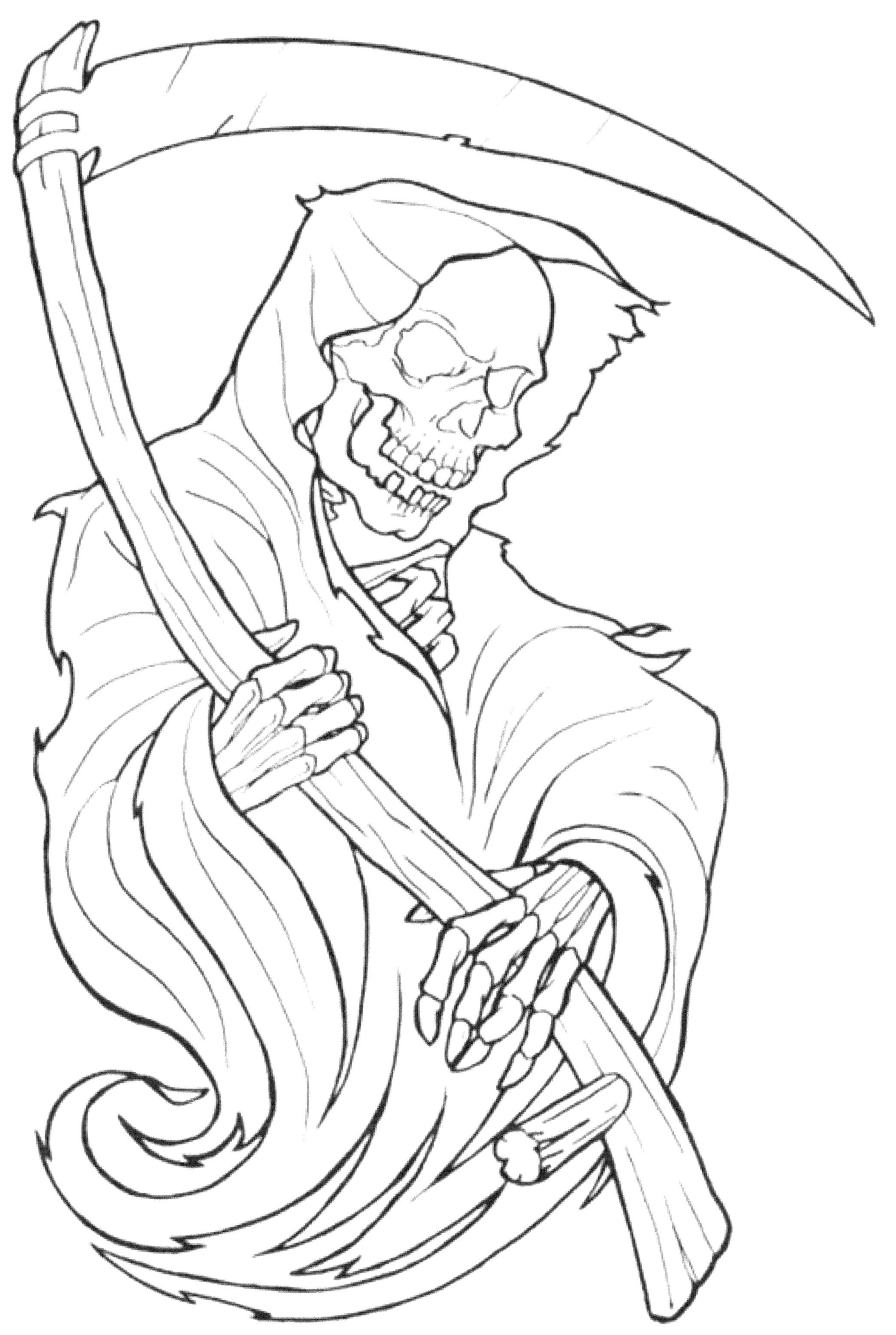

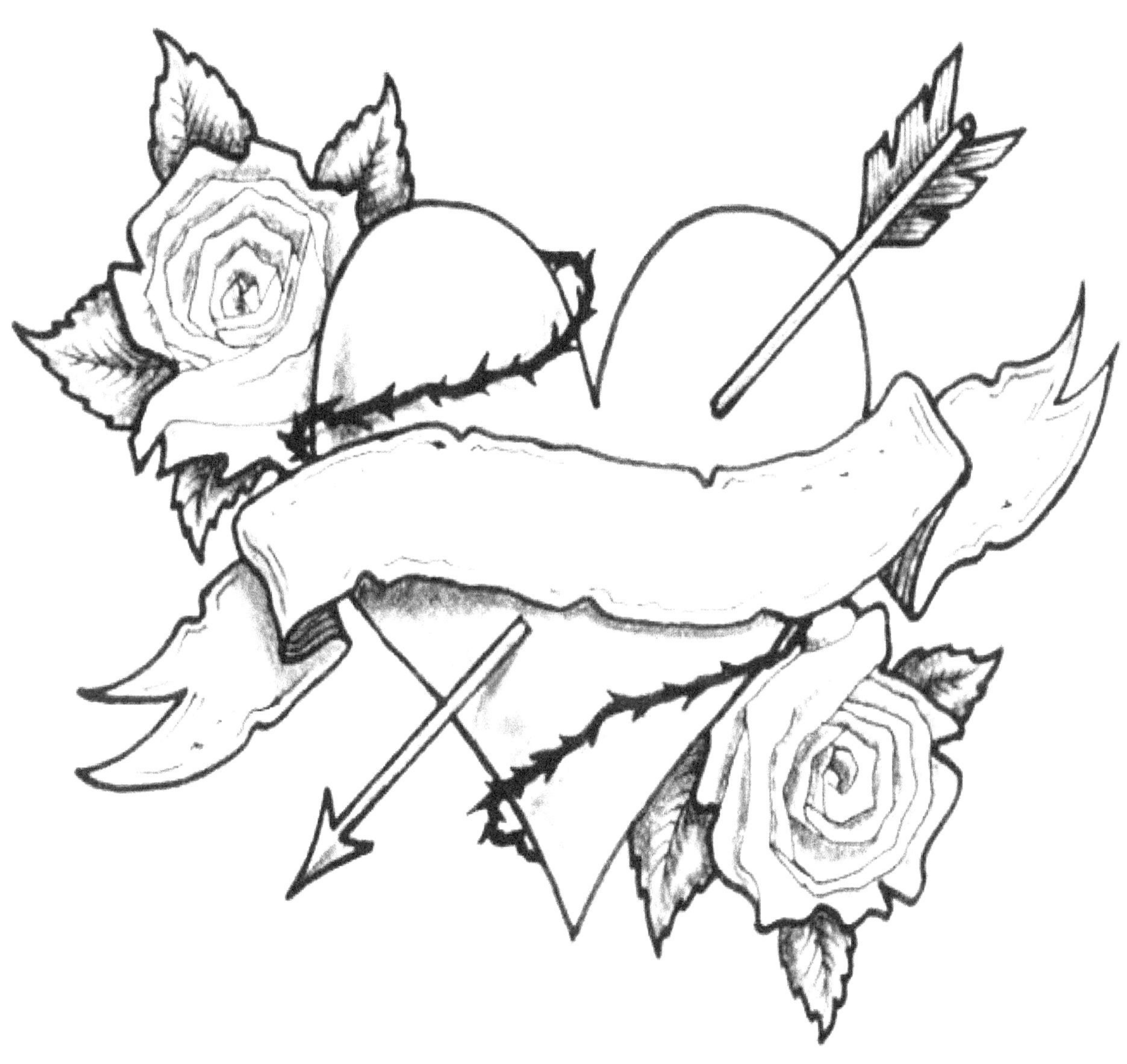

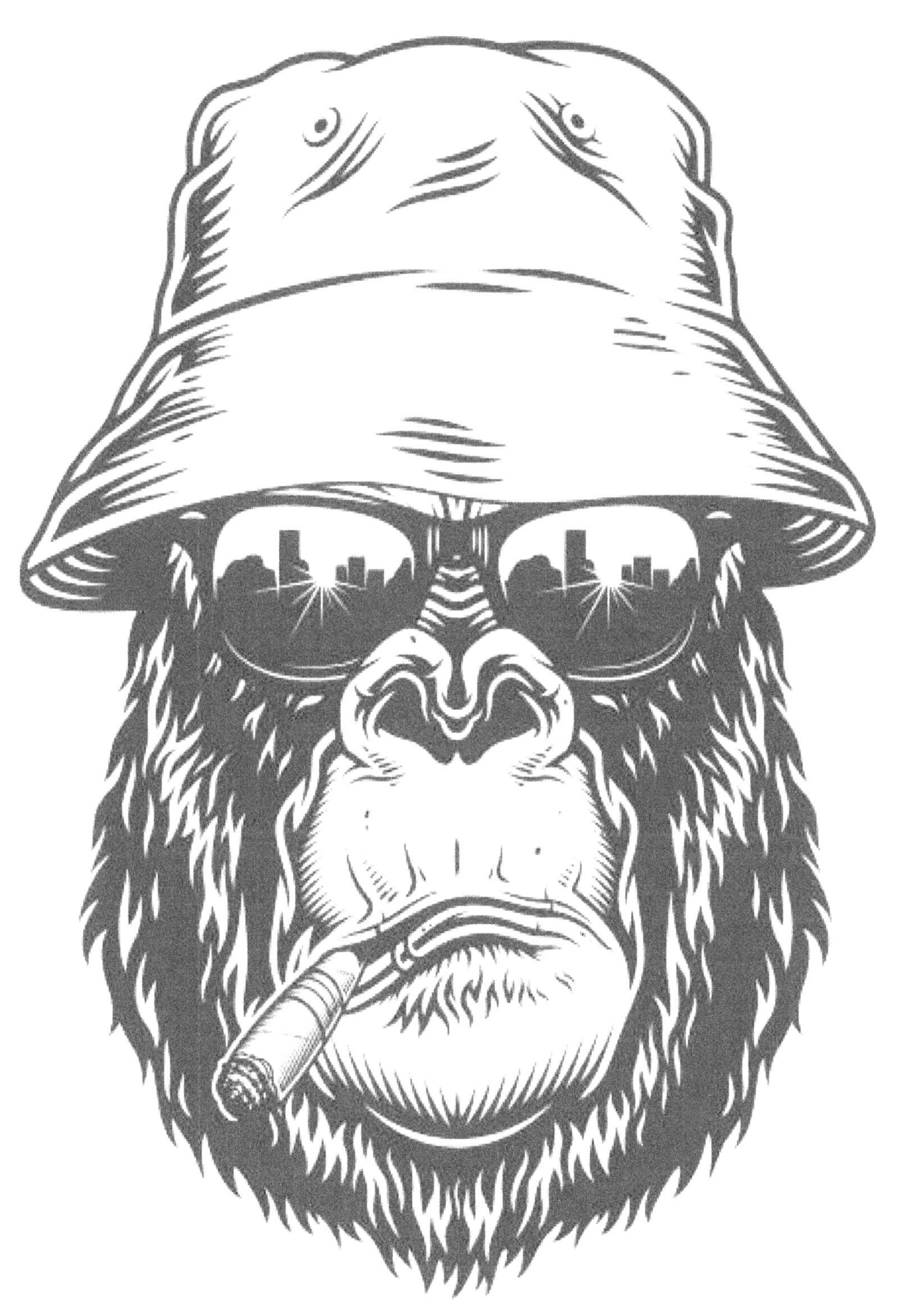

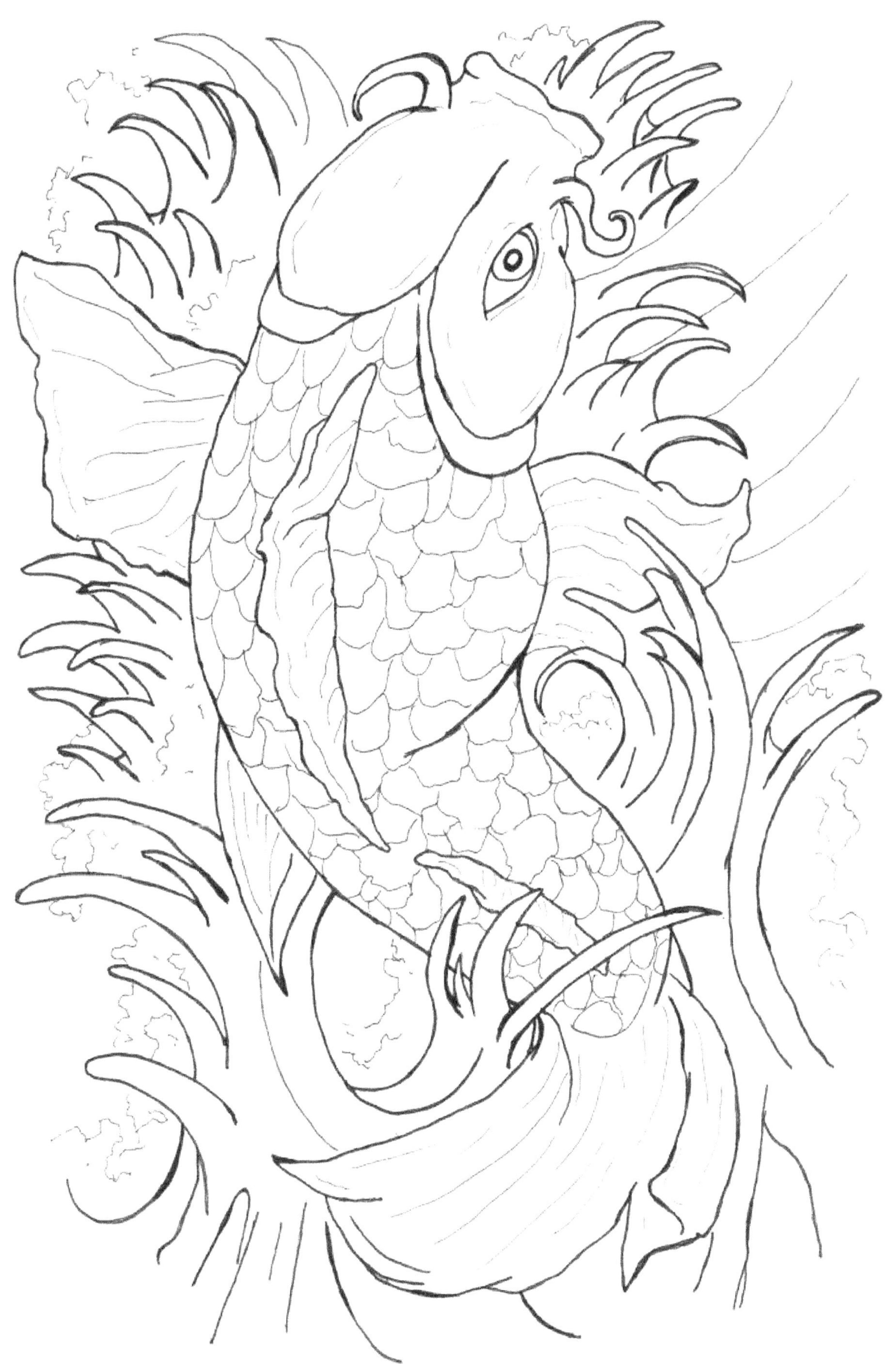

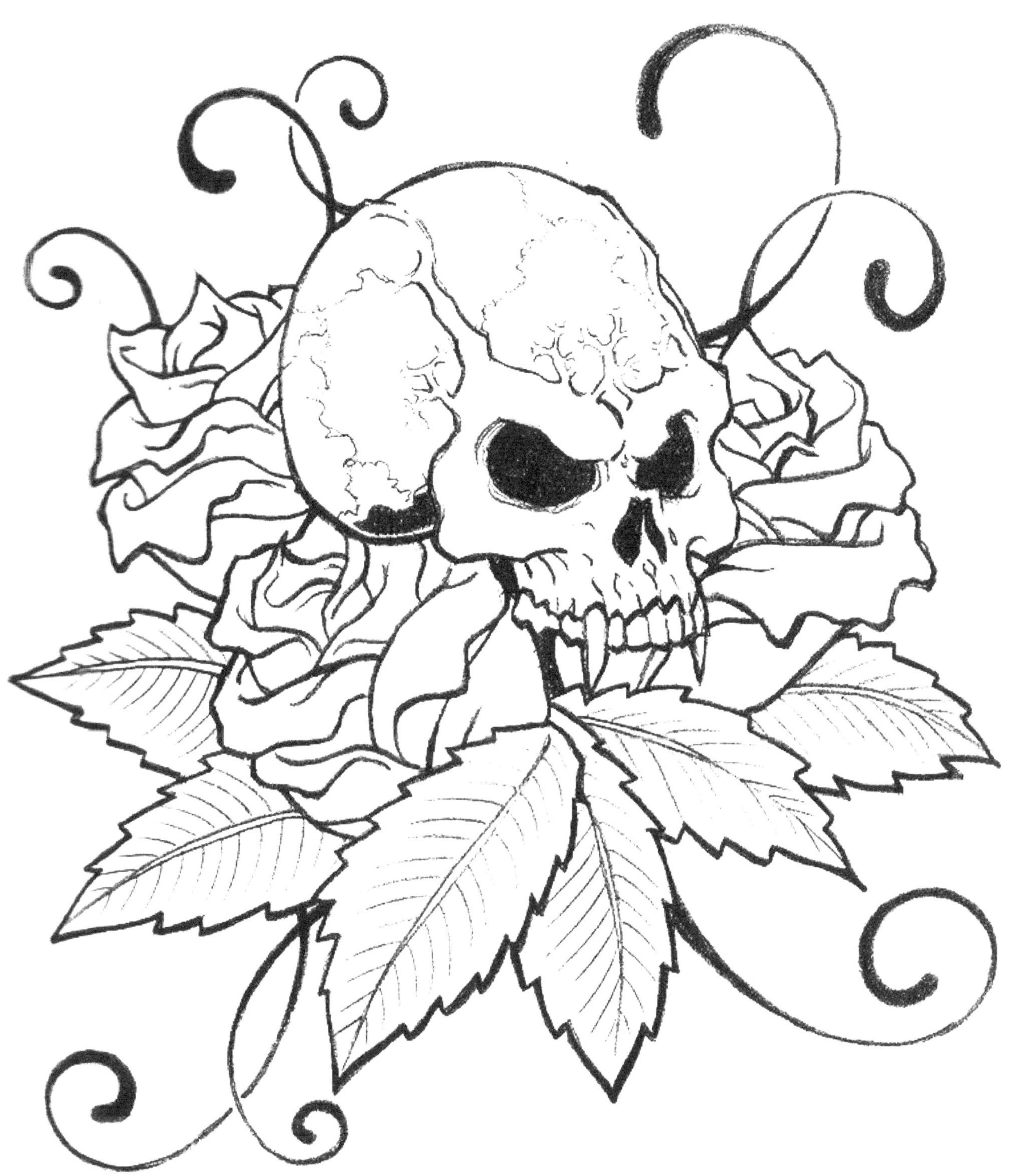

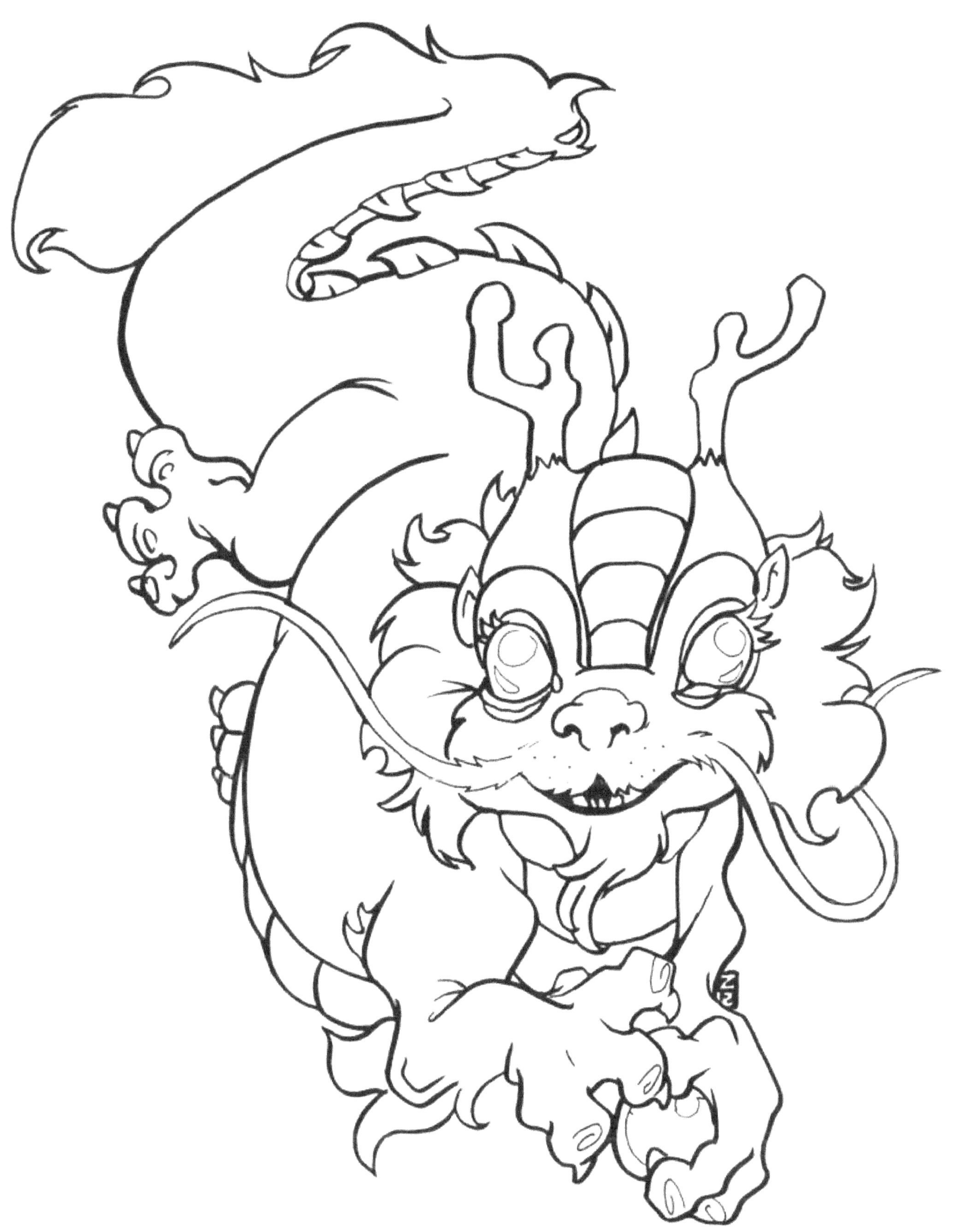

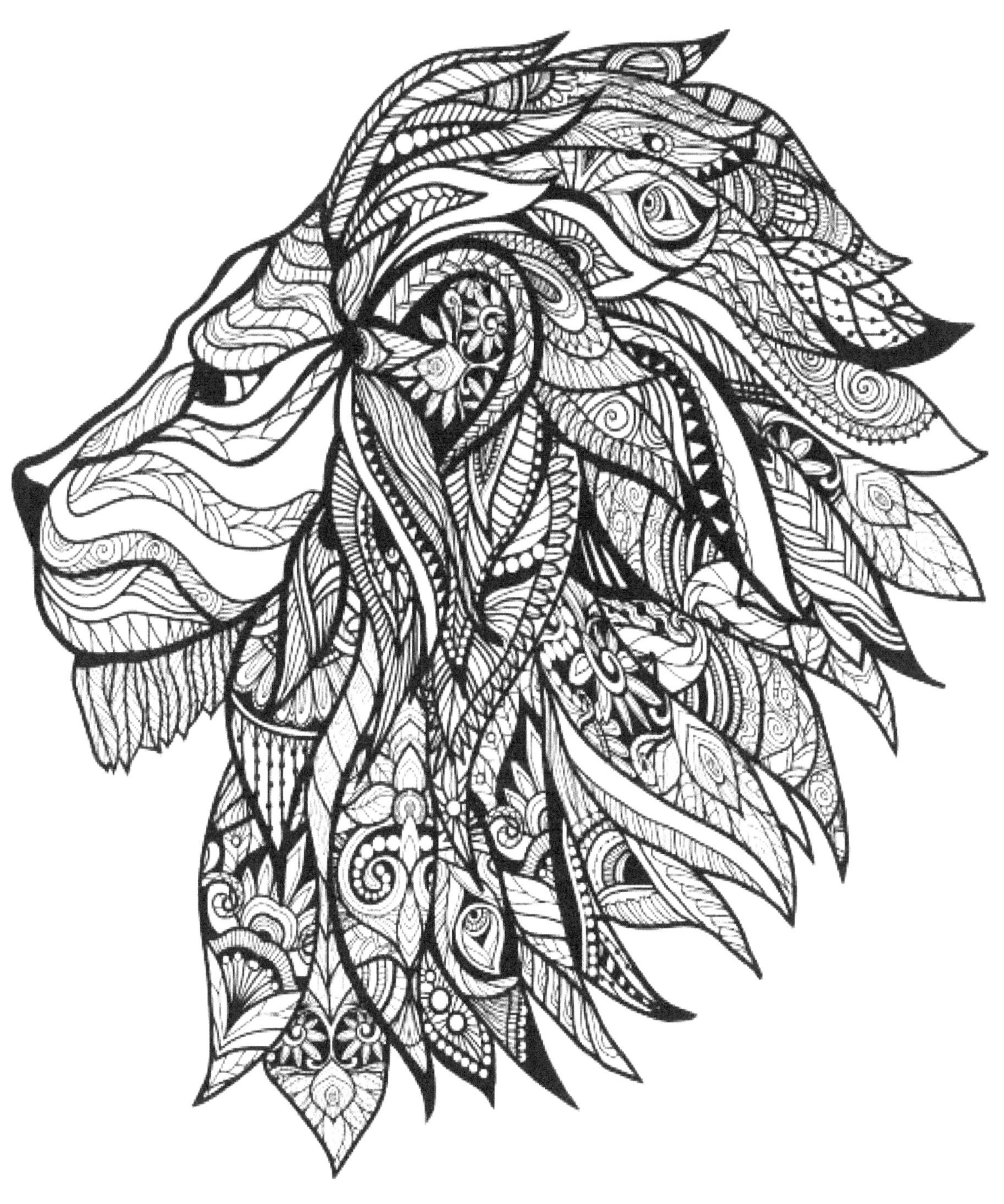

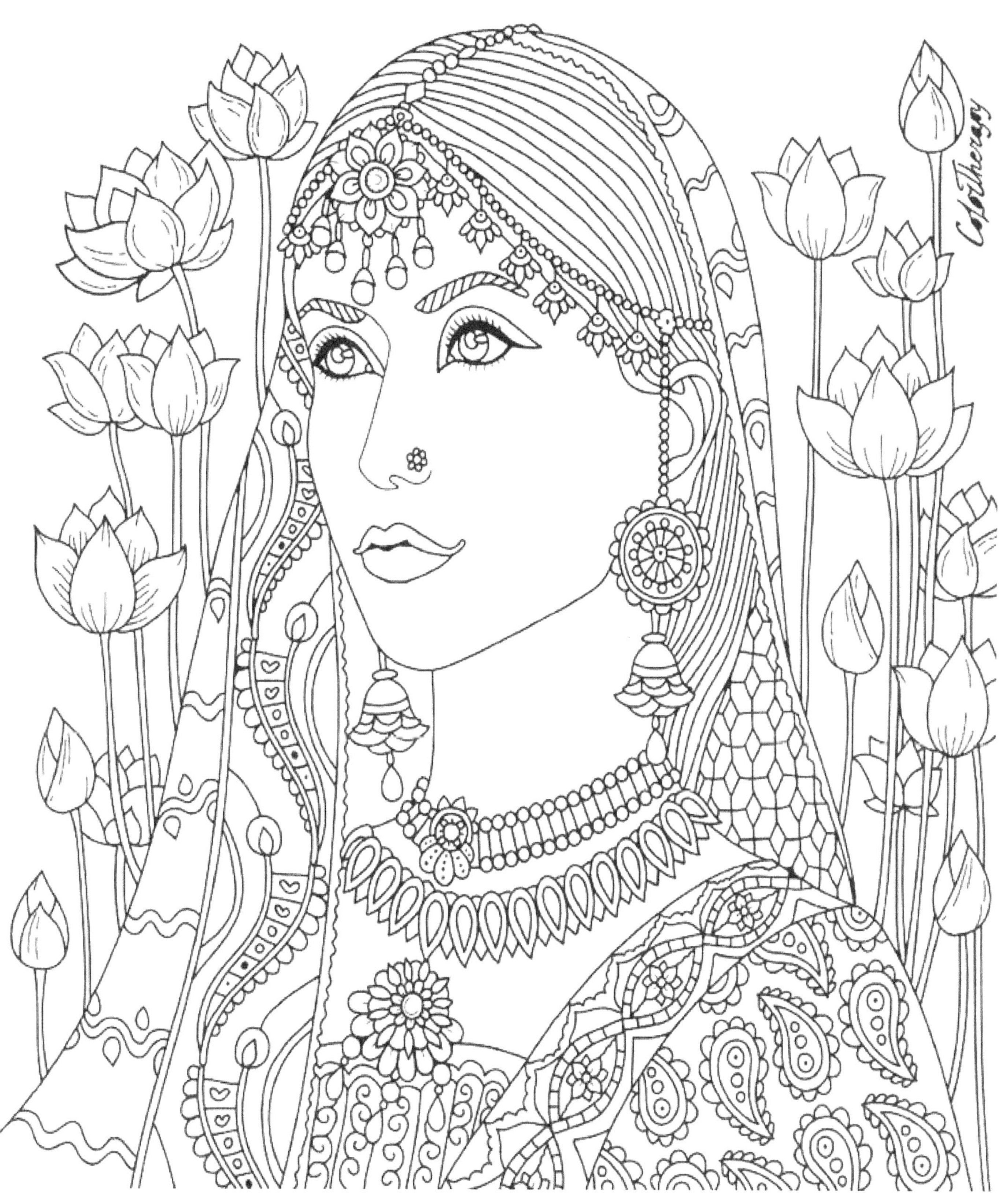

ColorTherapy

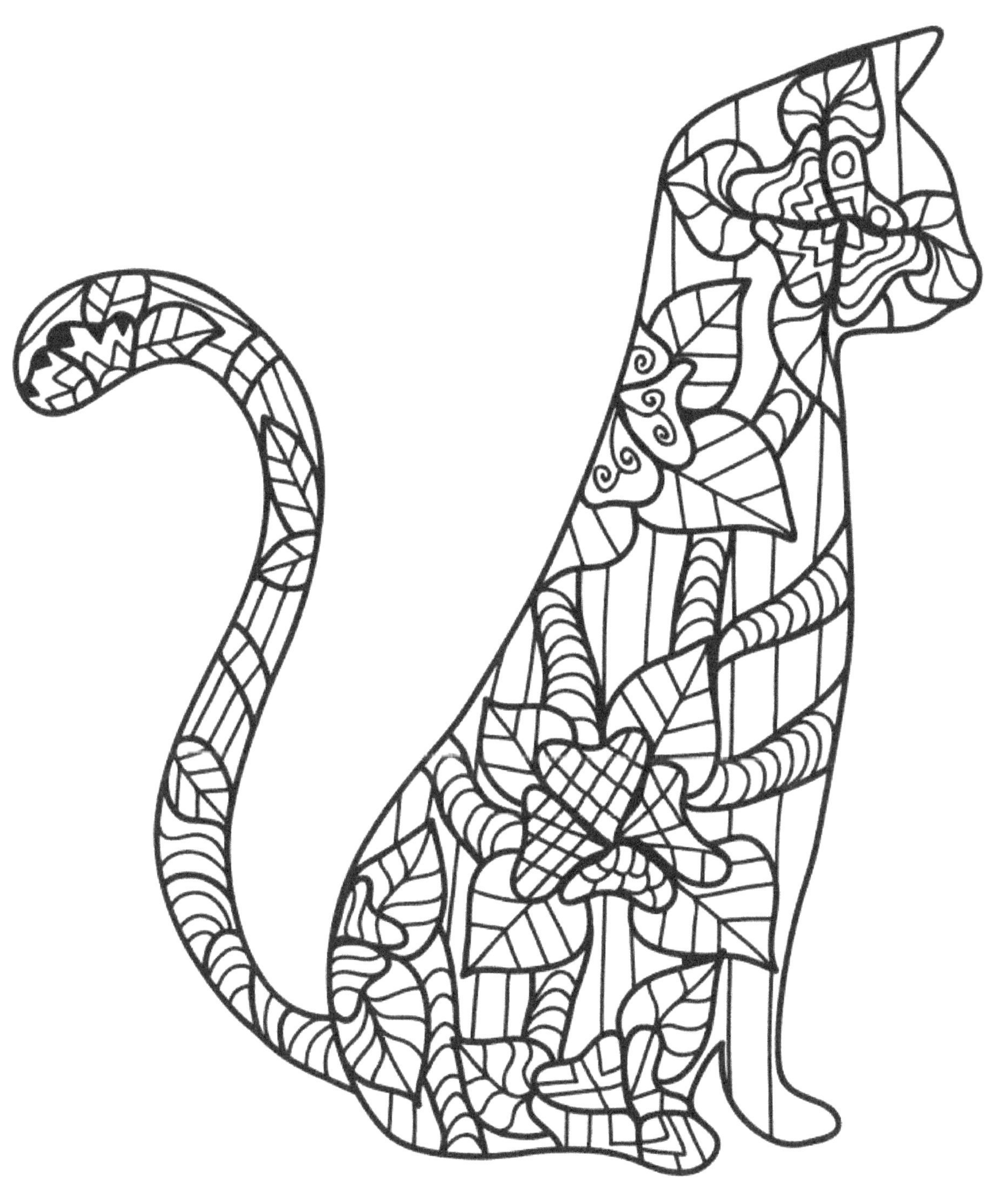

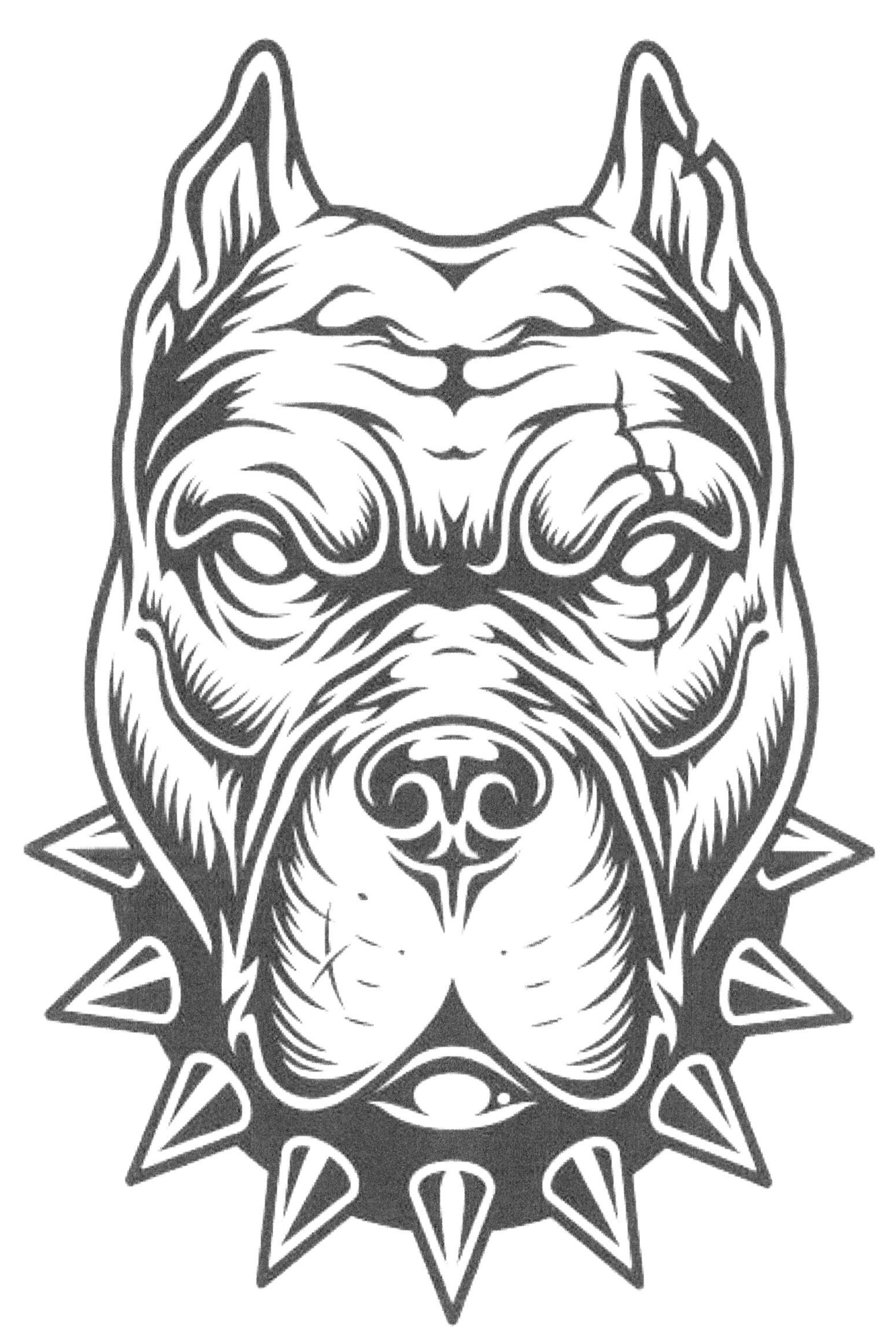

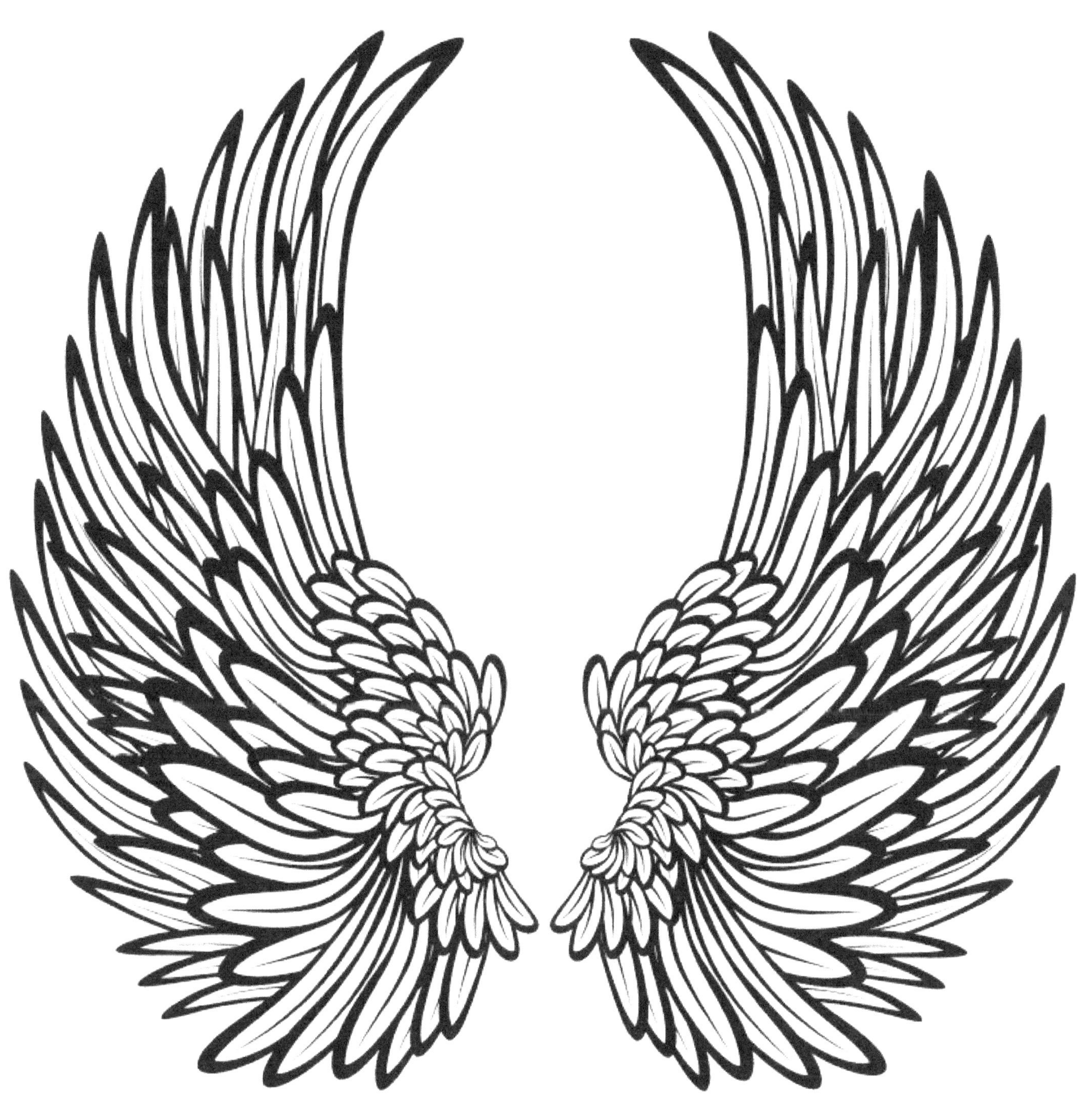

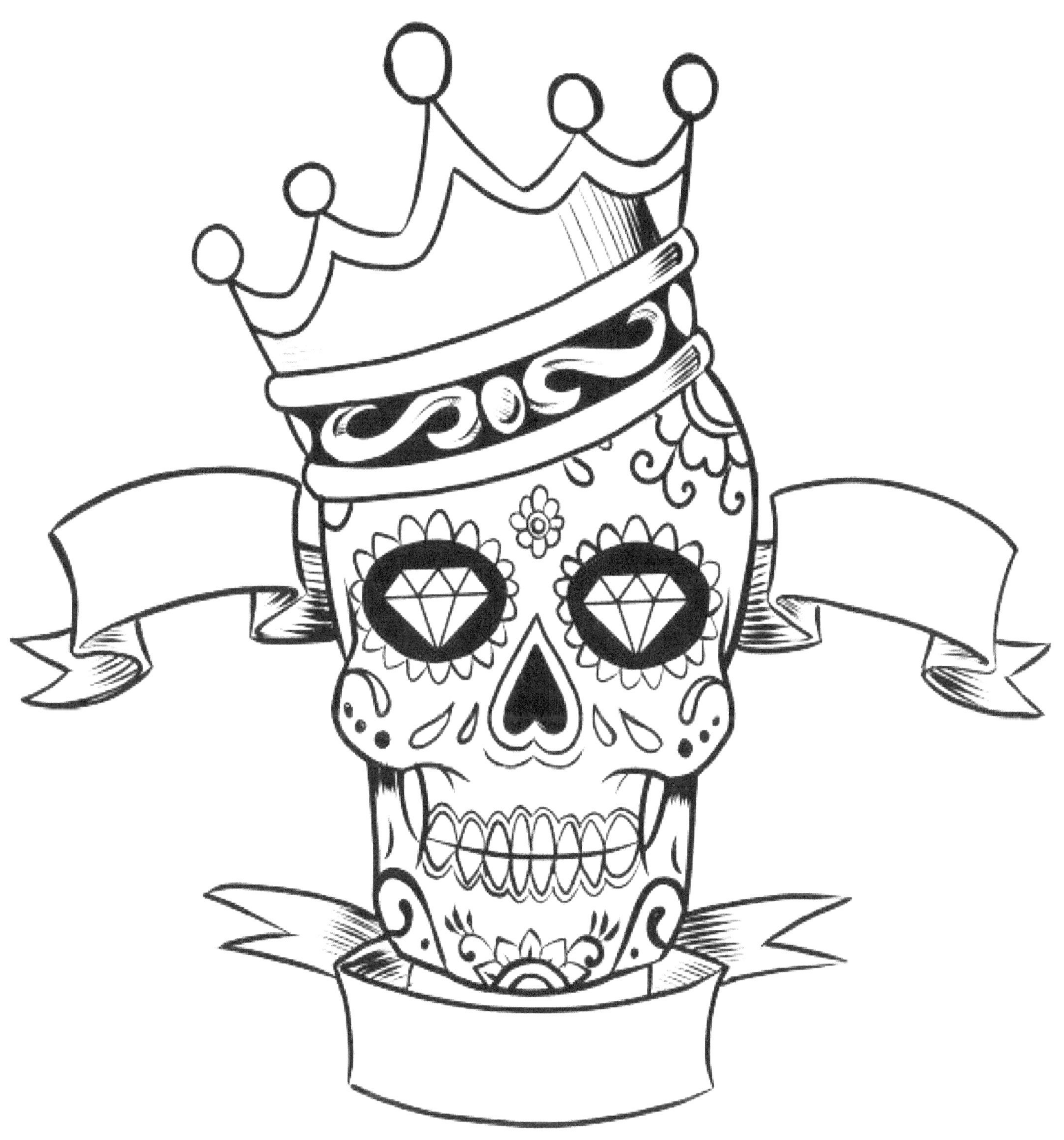

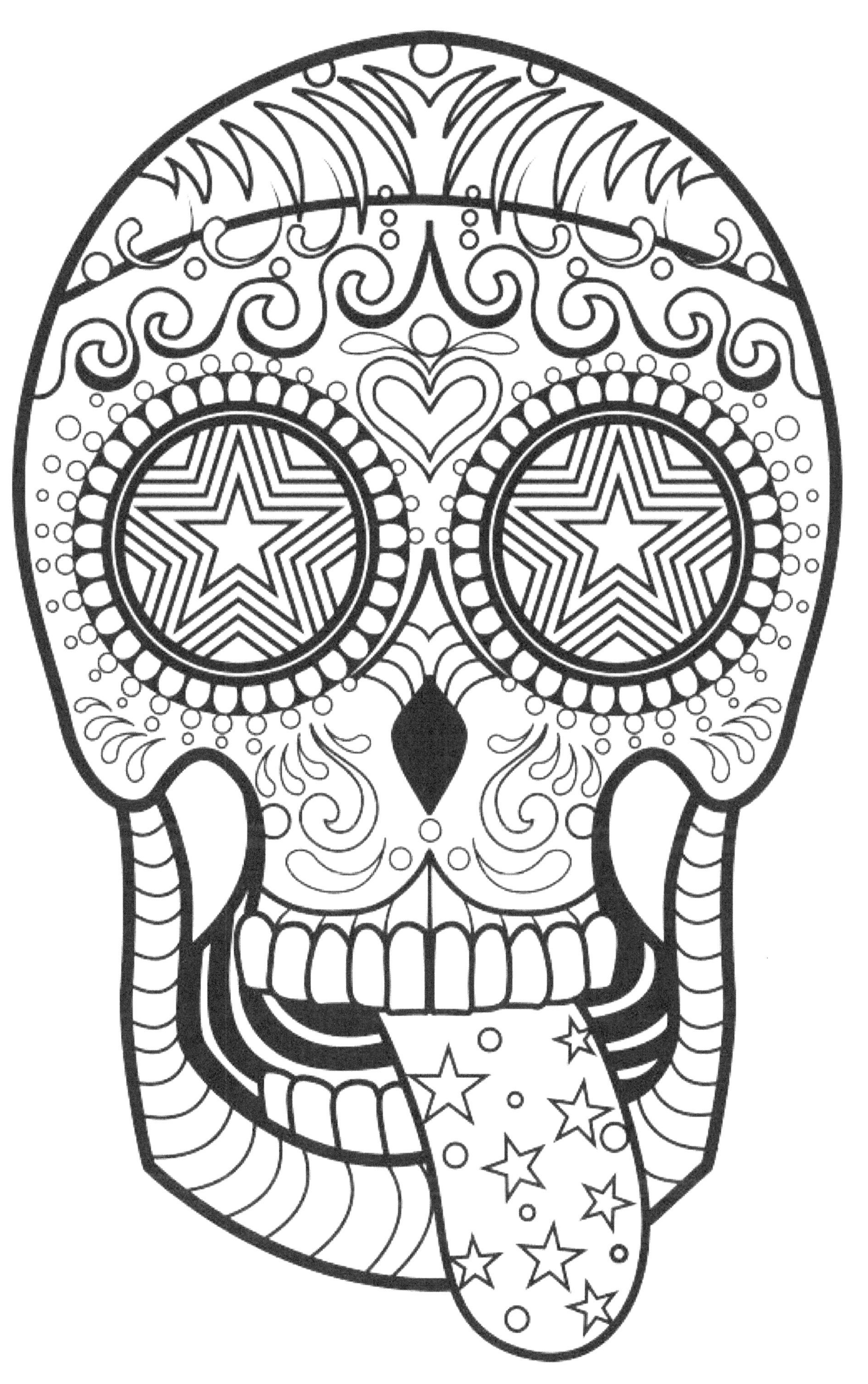

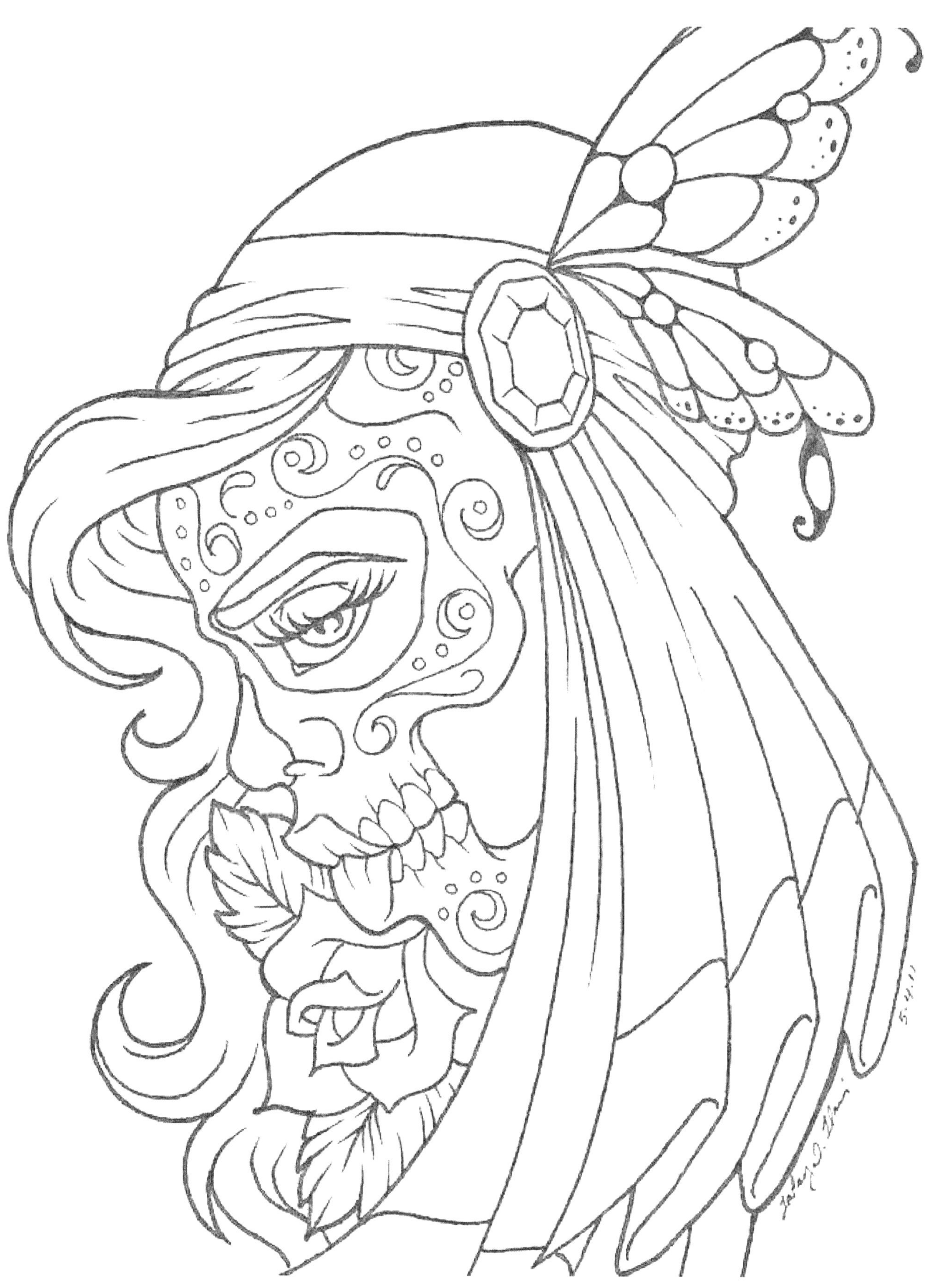

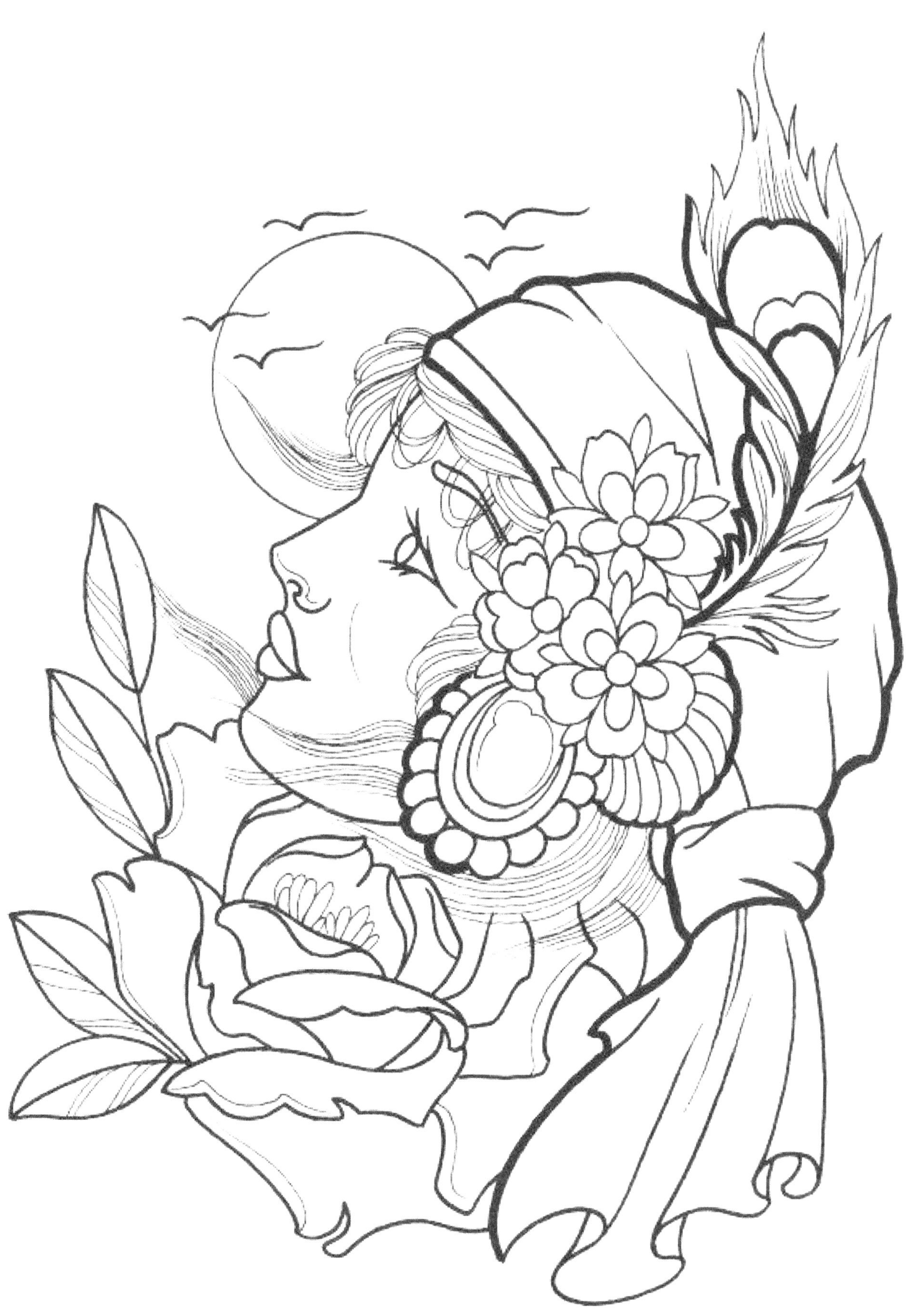

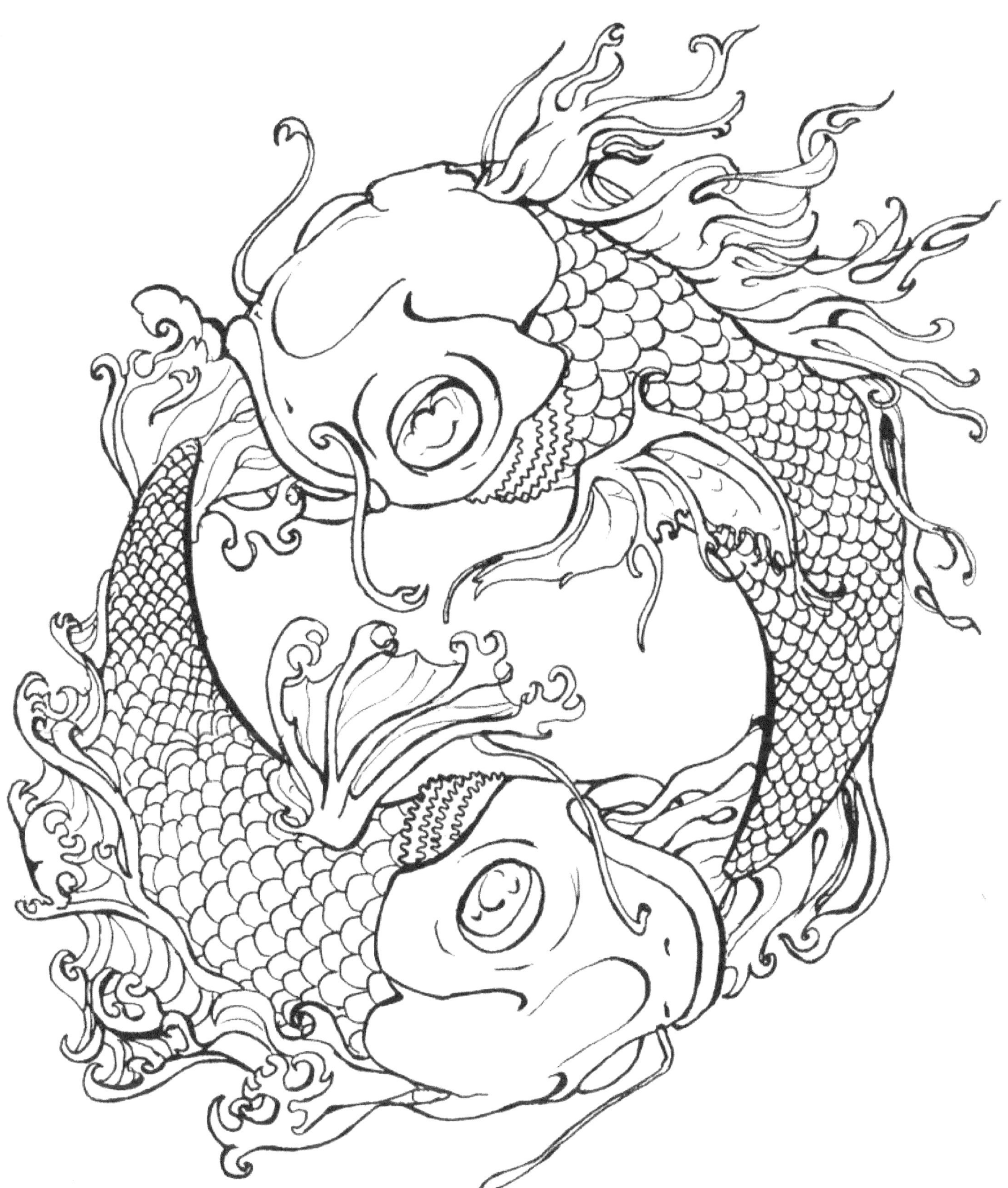

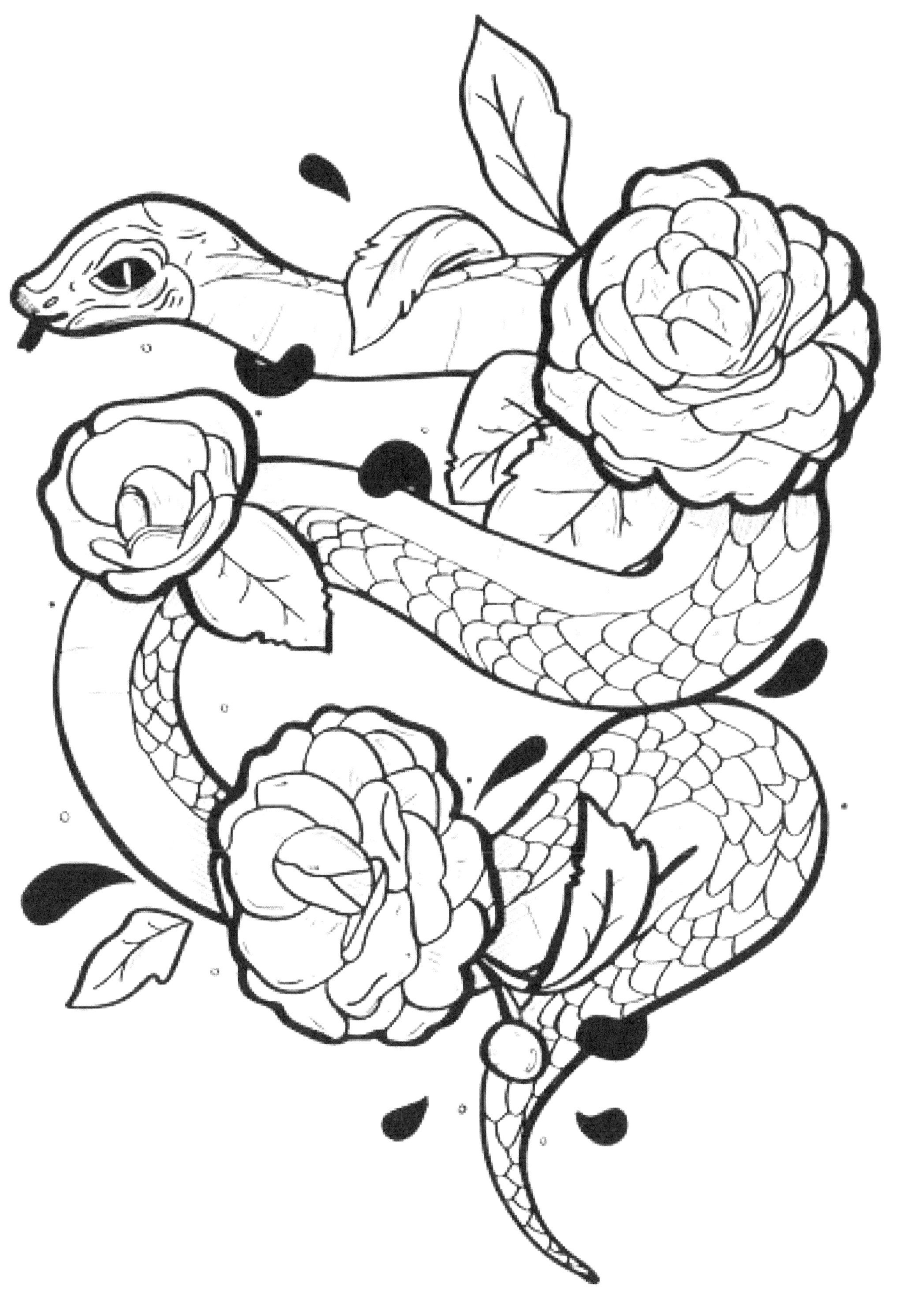

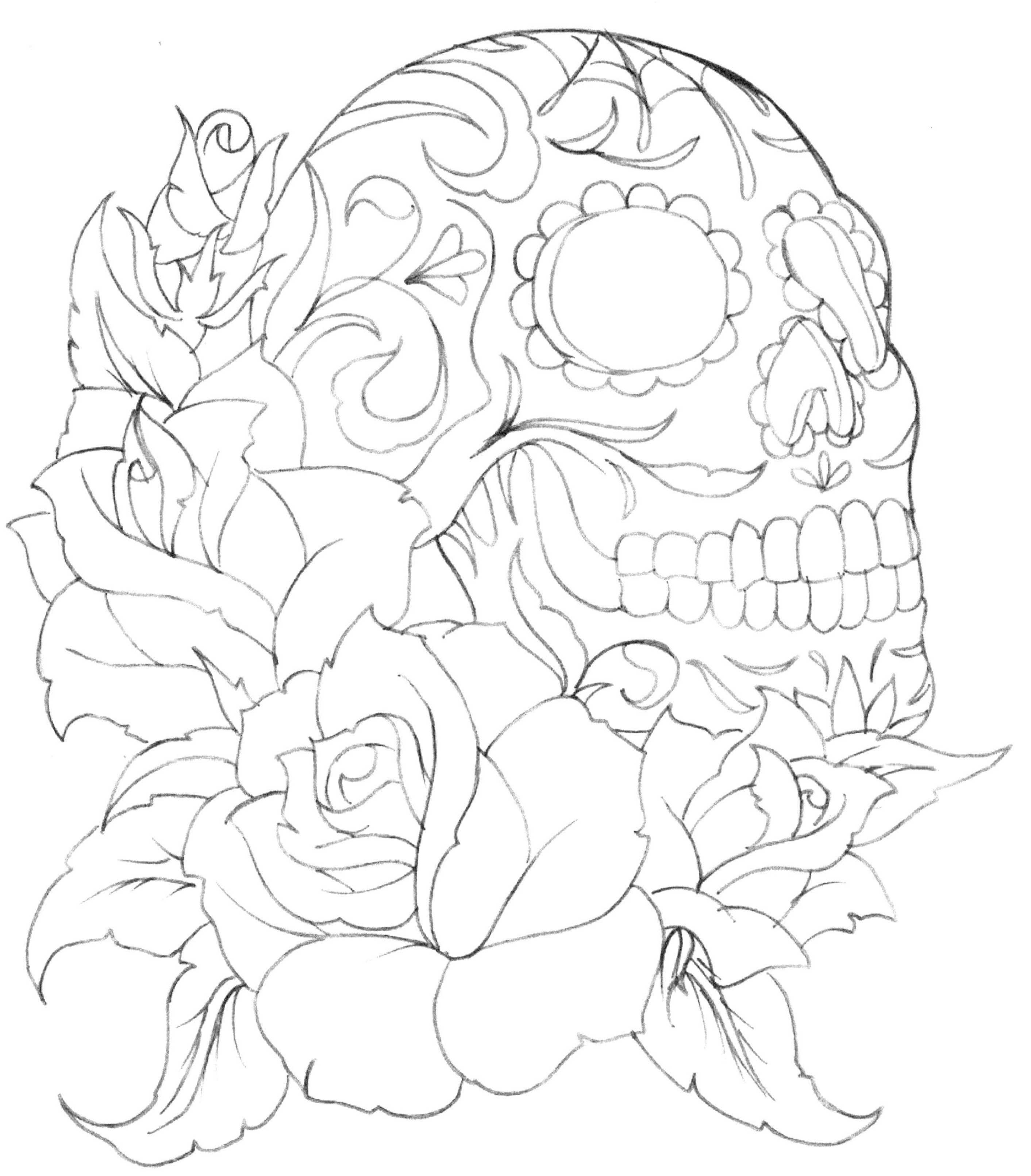

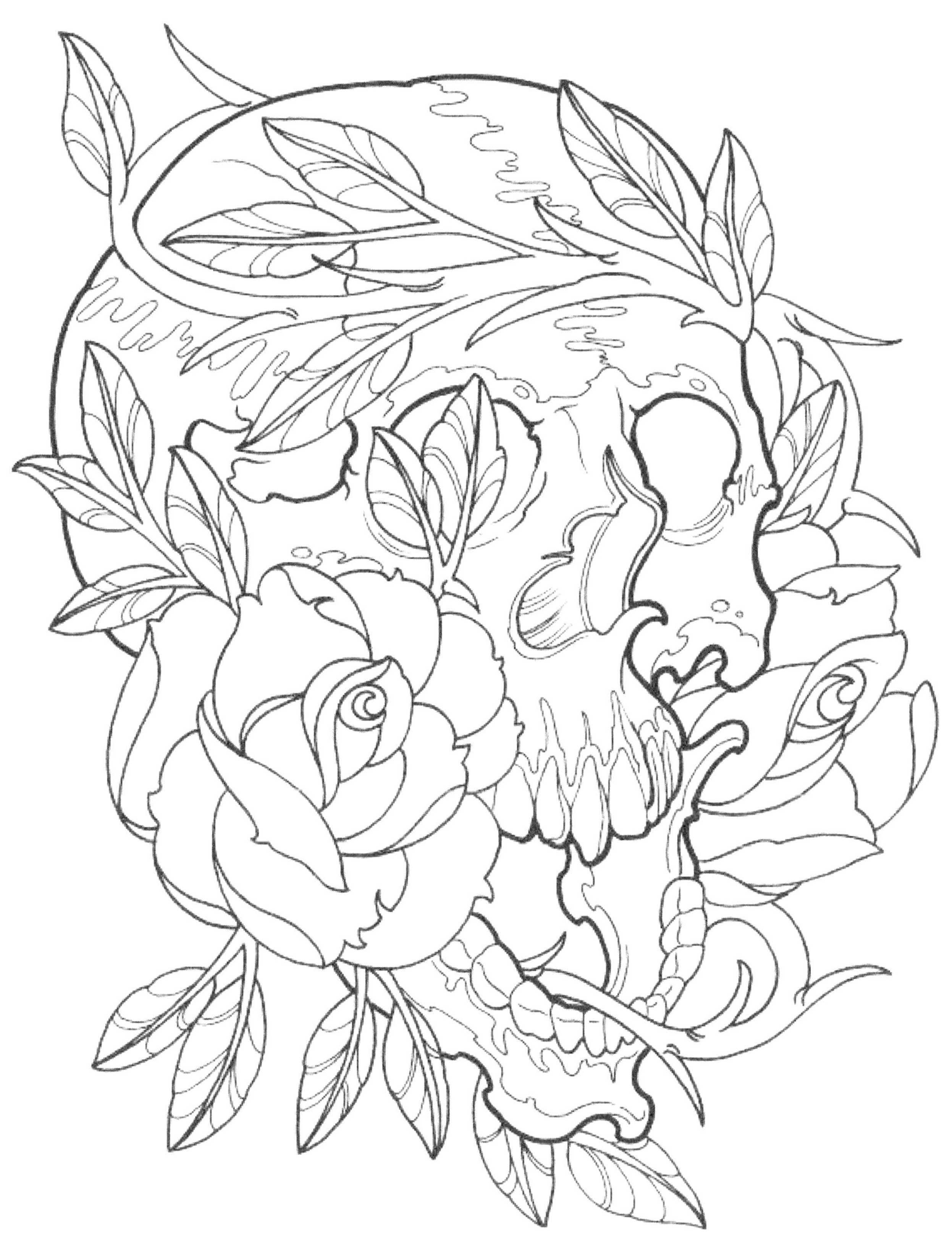

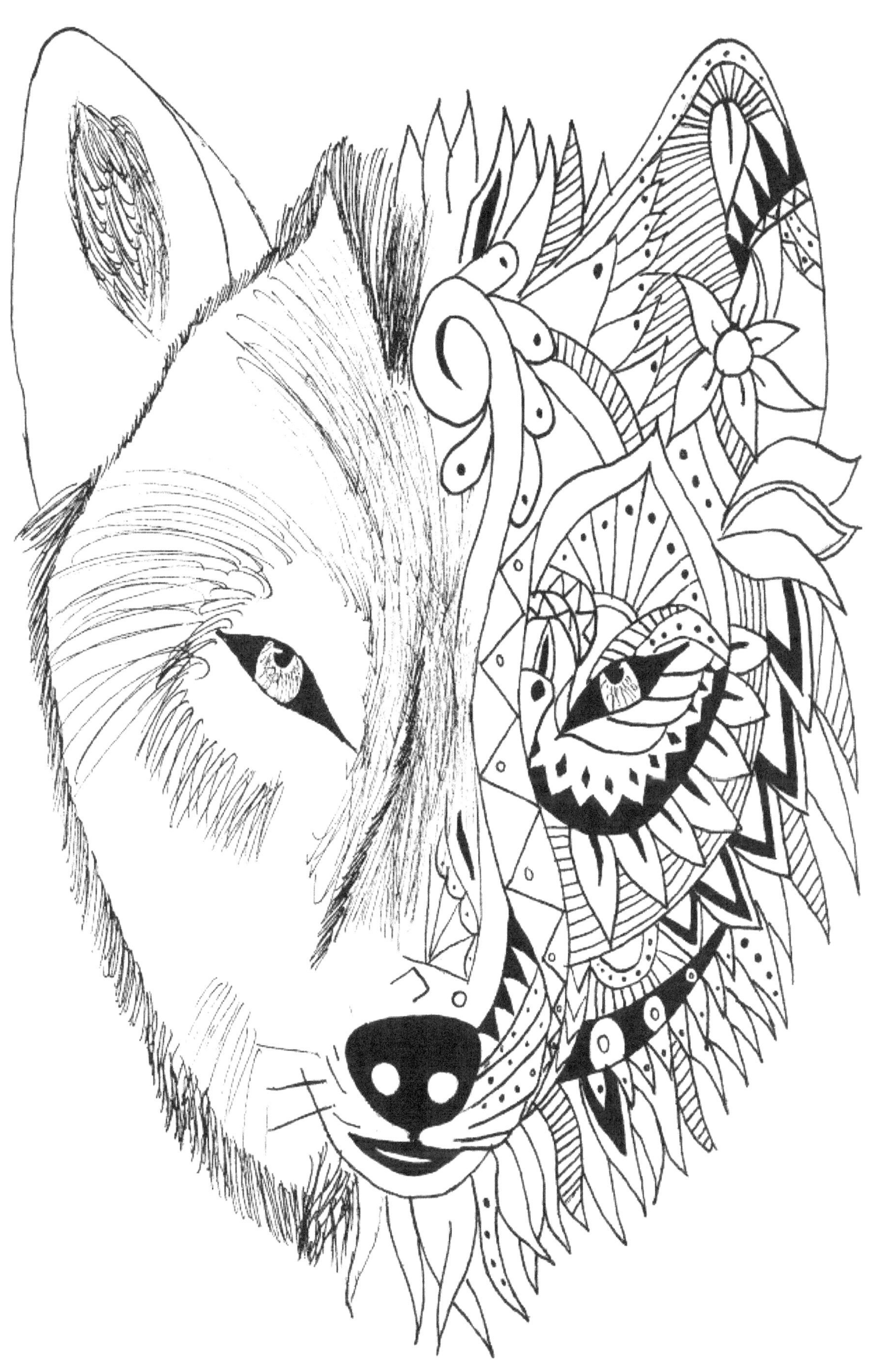

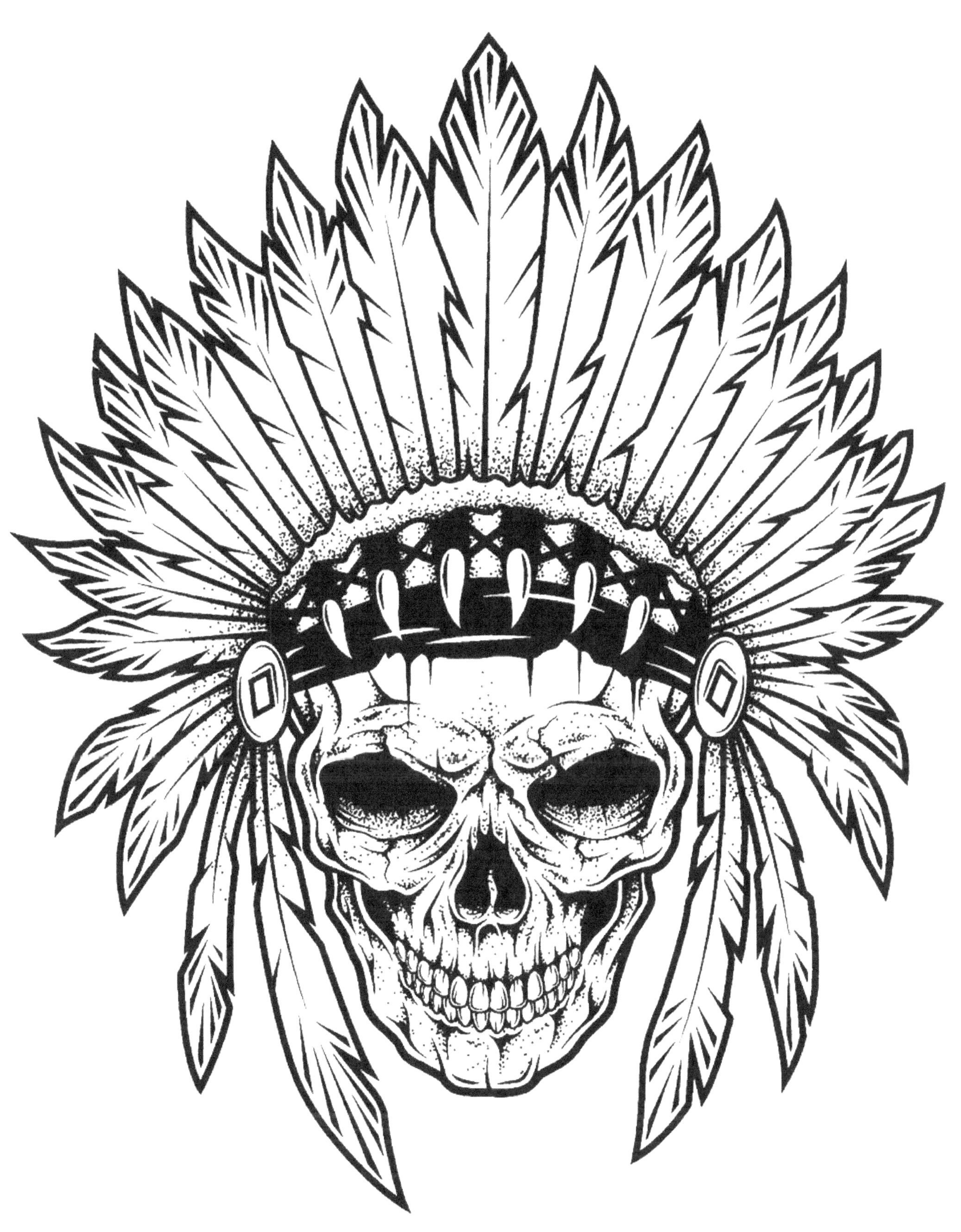

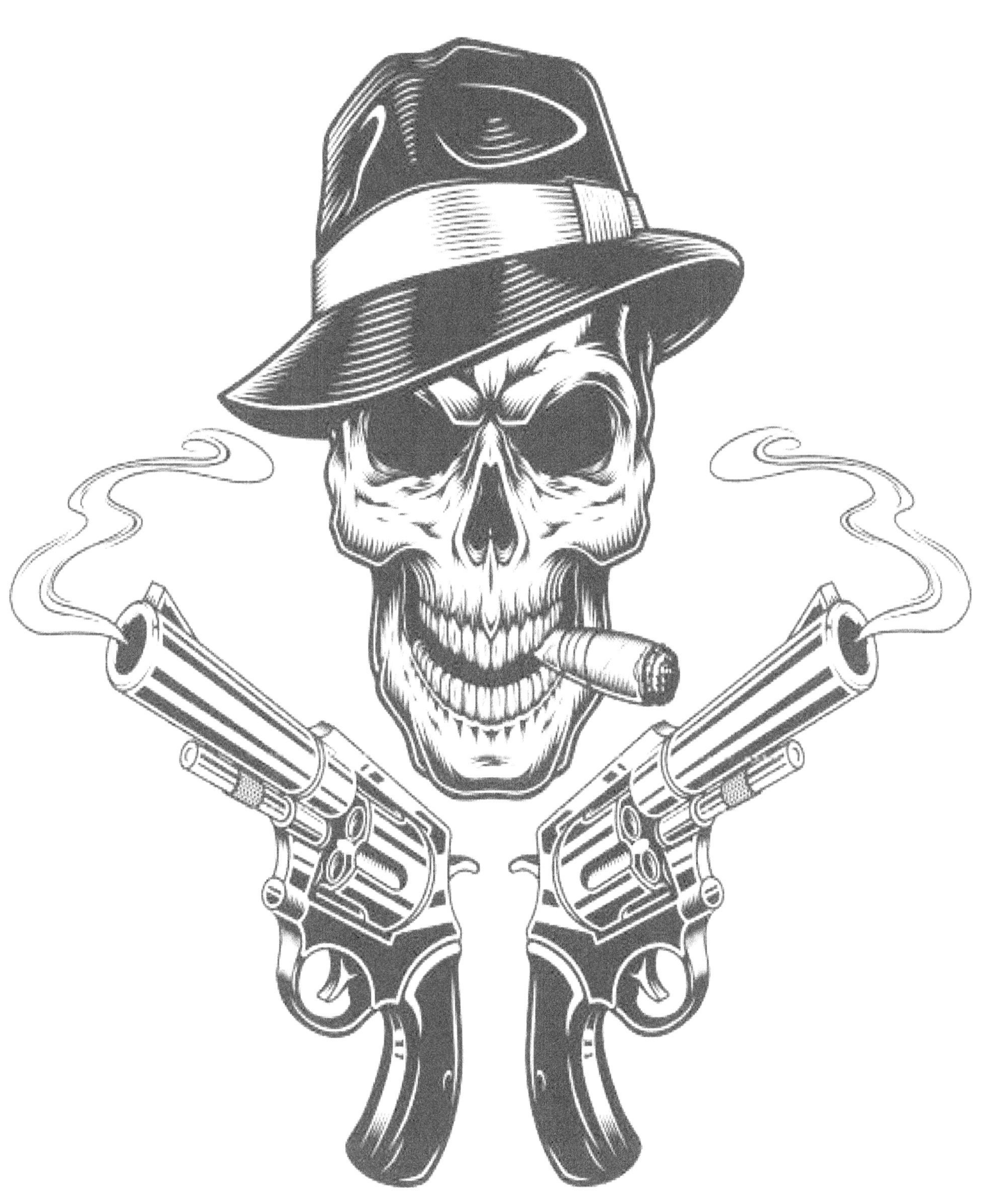

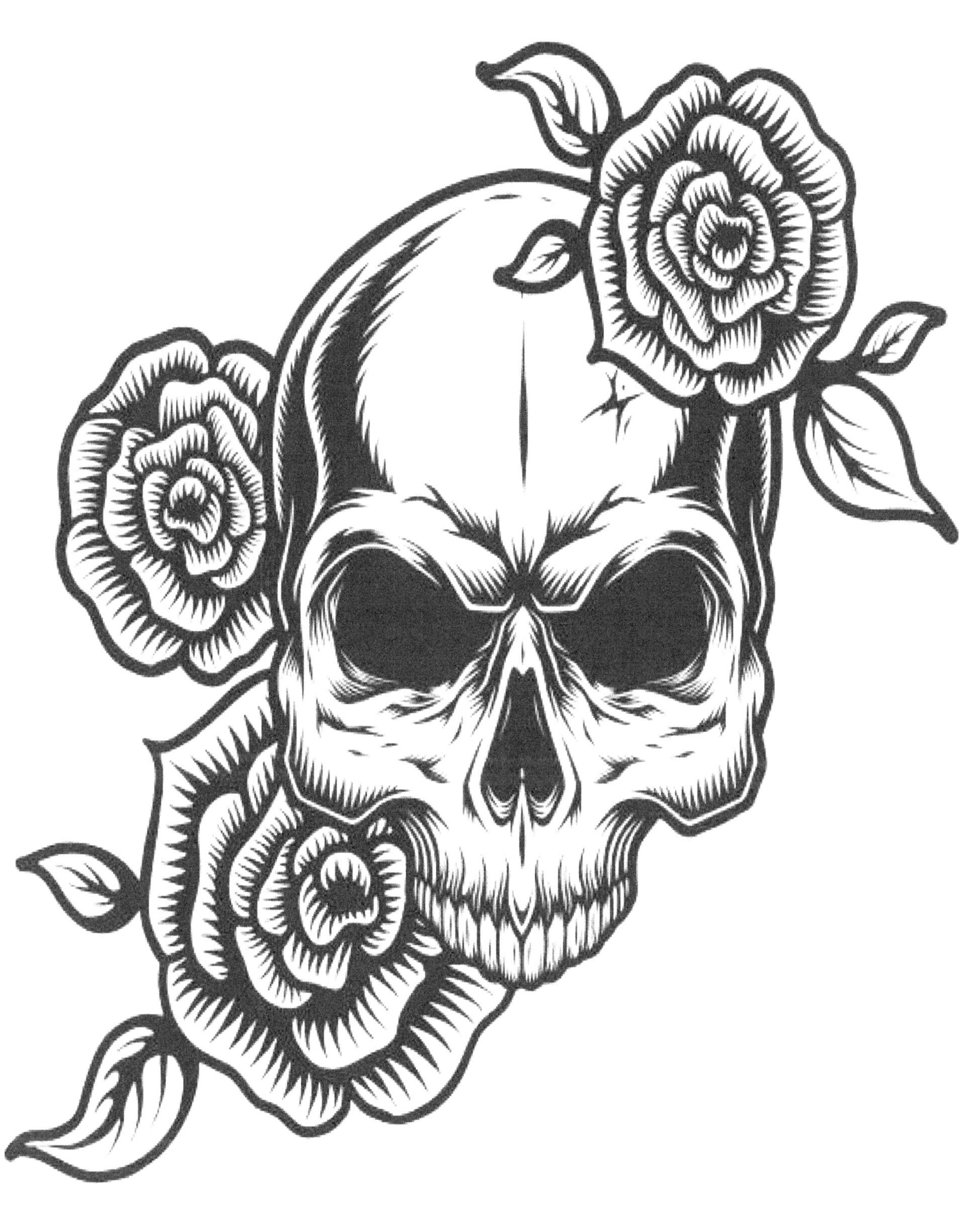

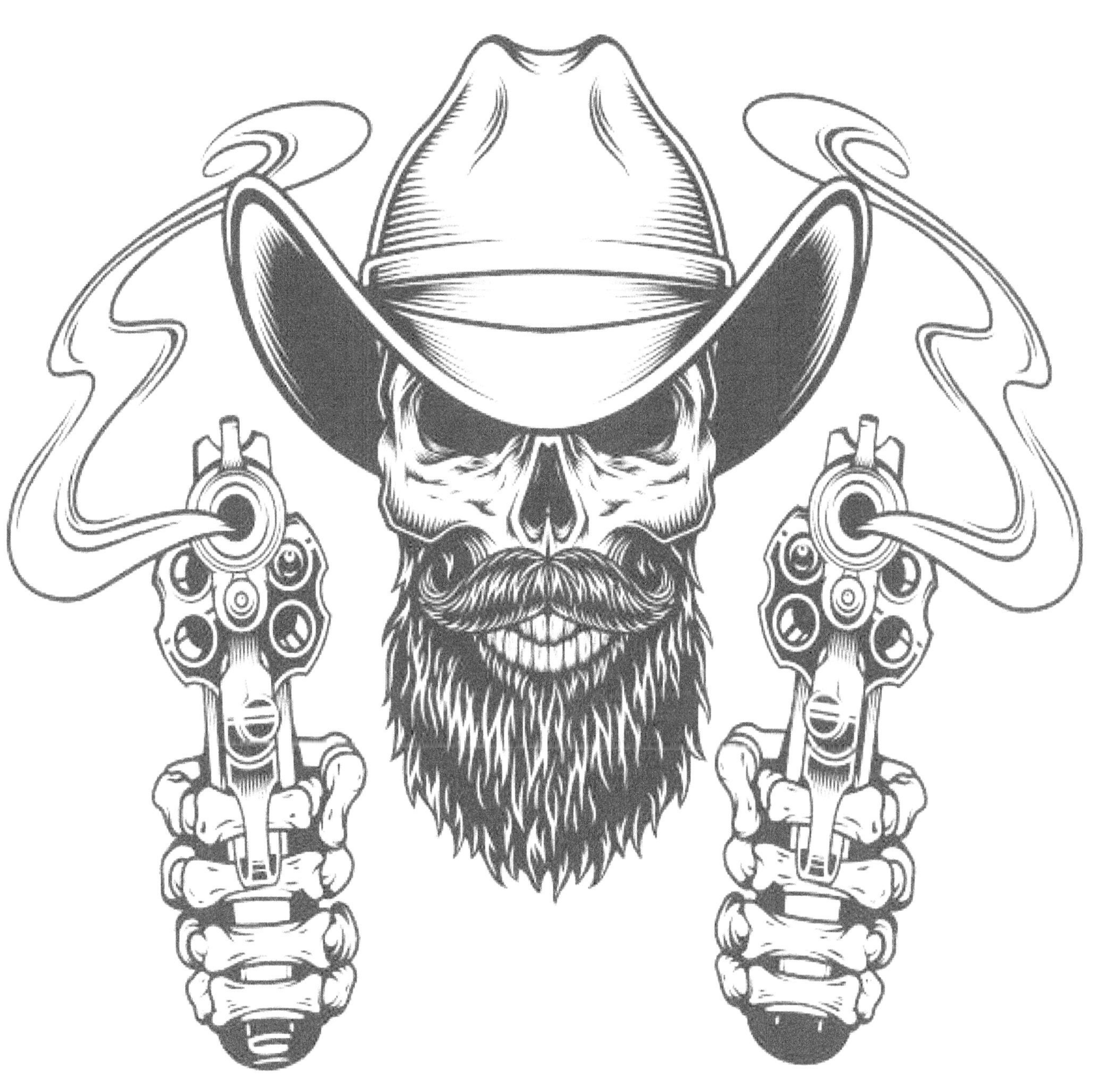